# The Three R's At Home

## Howard & Susan Richman

Pennsylvania Homeschoolers
R.D. 2 -- Box 117
Kittanning, PA 16201

Printed and Bound in the United States of America.

ISBN 0-929446-00-3

Library of Congress Catalog Card Number: 88-090813

2nd printing January 1, 1992

# Acknowledgments

Excerpt from *Escape from Childhood* by John Holt reprinted with permission of Holt Associates. Copyright by John Holt, 1974.

Excerpt from *Never Too Late: My Musical Life Story* by John Holt reprinted with permission of Holt Associates. Copyright by John Holt, 1980.

Excerpt from *The Phantom Tollbooth* by Norman Juster reprinted with permission of Random House. Copyright by Norman Juster, 1961.

Excerpts from *A Comprehensive Reading Communication Plan* (Working Edition), Spring 1979, by Morton Botel. Reprinted with permission of Morton Botel.

Thank you to Susannah Sheffer, editor of *Growing Without Schooling* for permission to reprint from the following articles written by Susan Richman which first appeared in *Growing Without Schooling*, copyright by Holt Associates:
  • "Playing With Math" by Susan Richman, Issue #25.

- "Coins, Jigsaw, & Cuisenaire" by Susan Richman, Issue #29.
- "On Young Children" by Susan Richman, Issue #44.
- "Vision Exercises Can Help" by Susan Richman, Issue #49.
- "The Process Behind Accomplishments" by Susan Richman, Issue #51.
- "Not Meant for Fun" by Susan Richman, Issue #57.
- "Comparing Tests" by Susan Richman, Issue #57.
- "We Think You Should Do It" by Susan Richman, Issue #58.
- "Studying History Together" by Susan Richman, Issue #62.

Back cover photograph of our family was taken by Bud Glendenning. Top row shows Susan and Howard; bottom row shows Molly, Hannah, Jacob and Jesse.

Illustrations are by the Richman children. Cover drawing of a house is by Jacob. Most of the inside drawings are by Jacob. Drawing of a girl reading "Dick and Jane" is by Molly.

Also thank you to Susannah Sheffer, Janice Richman, Nancy Chakovan, and Madalene Murphy for their help with editing this manuscript.

**To John Holt
who opened the door**

# Table of Contents

1. Introduction     **1**

     Susan's Background     **2**
     Howard's Background     **4**
     This Book     **6**

2. Reading to Children     **7**

     Reading With a Baby     **8**
     Reading to Answer Questions     **10**
     Science in Your Neighborhood     **13**
     Everything Has a Story     **16**
     Electricity Explorations     **17**
     The Soldier Game     **20**
     Civil War Times     **26**
     Home Economics     **31**
     Literary Appreciation     **34**

3. First Steps Toward Reading     **37**

     Learning to Read in School     **37**
     Learning to Read at Home     **39**
     Learning the Alphabet     **41**
     Learning The First Words     **45**
     Nicole Learns to Read Using Wordcards     **46**
     Simple Games for Learning Words     **48**
     A Short History of Reading Instruction     **50**
     Fun With Dick and Jane     **51**

4. Learning Phonics     **59**

     Dealing With Children's Frustrations     **60**
     Using a Phonics Program     **67**
     Molly and Jacob Learn Phonics Together     **72**
     Informal Phonics Lessons     **75**
     Discovering Phonics Ideas as an Adult     **78**

5. Helping Children Learn to Read     **81**

     Brian Teaches Himself to Read     **82**
     Bobby Learns to Read by Memorizing Words     **83**
     Emily Learns to Read at Age Two     **84**
     Christian Learns the Same Way     **85**
     Felicity Gets Inspired by a Gift     **87**

Jesse Begins to Read to Himself          89
Julie Reads When Her Mother Can't        91
Anita Learns to Read at Age Twelve       93
Nathan Gets to the Top of the Mountain   95

6. First Steps Toward Writing            99

Jesse Begins Sound-Spelling              100
Jacob and Molly Begin Sound-Spelling     108

7. Becoming a Writer                     113

Writer's Voice                           113
Putting out a Newspaper                  115
Making Books                             120
Rough Drafts                             125
Editing on the Computer                  126
Write From The Start                     129
Other Good Books on Writing              133

8. Math                                  135

Measurement and Shapes                   135
Math and Money                           137
Approaching Math Through History         138
Starting Out With Cuisenaire Rods        143
Doing Math Work                          148
Using a Math Textbook                    155
Math in the Real World                   159
Math in Real Books                       160

9. Tests and Records                     163

Homeschooled Children Score High         167
Preparing for Standardized Tests         169
Jesse's Experience With Tests            171
Keeping Records                          175

10. Writing Our Own Curriculum           181

On Serendipity and Homeschooling         182
Writing a Curriculum                     184
List Resources                           186
Put a Coat and Tie on it                 188
Specify Evaluation Measures              189
Jesse's Fourth Grade Curriculum          190

11. Getting Organized                    197

Feeling Stressed-Out                                 197
Organizing the Homeschooling Day                     202
Getting Rid of the Big Time Waster                   205
Scheduling Time for Dad With Kids                    207
Sibling's Special Time with Each Other               213
Moving Towards Positive Traditions                   215

12. What We Have Learned                             223
Reading Aloud is the Foundation                      223
First Steps Must Not Be Rushed                       223
Finding a Regular Rhythm                             224
Keep Sessions Enjoyable                              224
Use Real Life Situations                             226
Recognize Accomplishments                            226
Establish a Collegial Relationship                   227
In Sum                                               228

# 1. Introduction

This book is for homeschooling parents who are looking for new ideas for opening up reading, writing, and mathematics for their children, and for people who are thinking about teaching their own children but want an inside look at how some families are doing things.

Many parts of this book first appeared in the journal Howard and I edit, *Pennsylvania Homeschoolers*, or the late John Holt's magazine, *Growing Without Schooling*. We wish to thank Susannah Sheffer, the editor of *Growing Without Schooling* for permission to reprint from our many contributions to that excellent journal.

**This book is written in two type fonts. Susan's writing is in ordinary print while mine is in boldface. While putting this book together has been a true joint effort, we each certainly have our own voices and we thought you'd want to know who was doing the "talking" as you're reading along. Also, as you can imagine, when one of us is typing, the other is with the children.**

**We have been homeschooling for ten years , in the long view, as our kids have never attended school. Our children are Jesse, 10; Jacob, 7; Molly 4; and Hannah, 6 months, and you'll be hearing lots about all of them. We hope you won't be confused that they will appear at all different ages throughout the book. Many parts of chapters were first written when they were a bit younger, and we decided to keep the original and immediate feel of those pieces.**

## Susan's Background

Ten years ago this summer our son Jesse was born, and that's also when I officially dropped out of school teaching. I was always something of a misfit as a teacher in schools, but I didn't quite know then that I'd find my niche as a parent, teaching and learning with my own kids at home. By the time he was 2 1/2, Jesse was firmly announcing that he'd never go to school -- no nursery school, no preschool, not the school where his father taught. No school. About that time I was visiting my mother in Georgia and happened to catch John Holt on The Donahue Show. I remember my sister and mother saying with disgust, "Oh no! Just see what that crazy John Holt is up to now! Have you ever heard of anything so ridiculous?" I admit the idea did sound somewhat ridiculous to me then, but I couldn't get the thought out of my head. Homeschooling -- no school. At all. Ever. Continuing to learn with my kids. No rigmarole of trying to set up our own alternative school, with worries about money and staffing.

Soon afterward I found *Growing Without Schooling*, the journal founded by the late John Holt, found one friend who was seriously contemplating the whole idea, and after awhile I convinced Howard that we should do it. He finally realized how much it meant to me, and that it wasn't one of those decisions that you could come back to in eighteen years. Jesse of course needed no convincing at all -- he'd held firm to his earlier feelings about schooling.

It's funny to think of how we fell into doing a state homeschooling newsletter. In March of 1982 I was riding with a friend down to see John Holt at a Pittsburgh television studio. She began saying how nice it would be if someone would gather the names and addresses of everyone in the audience that day. I agreed wholeheartedly. Then she said someone could even send out copies of that list, so we could all stay in touch. Again I said, "Great idea." She continued, saying it might also be nice if someone could have a file of sample curriculums and letters people had written to their school districts. I agreed again, thinking of course that *she* was thinking of doing all this herself. I was trying to encourage her in it. Then she added that maybe someone could periodically write up something about what was available in the file and send it out -- like, perhaps, a sort of newsletter. Again I told her that was a great idea. Then she looked me square in the eye and said, "And we all think YOU should be the one to do it!" What could I say but, "Great idea!" And so it began -- a little two-page notice at first, then five pages, then we began getting more responses from readers and more contacts from new folks, and things just grew and grew. As a friend told me, I've really found my niche now.

I sometimes look back at myself as a paid teacher in schools and shudder. I was so green, so unaware, so young. I fancied myself as someone who liked to read aloud to groups of kids, for example, and felt I did it pretty well. But though I tried to stock my classroom with good books, the truth is that I had never read most of them. Or at least hadn't read them like a *parent* reads children's books, over and over again until you know every nuance of *Mike Mulligan and His Steam Shovel* or *Frog and Toad are Friends*. Not like a parent who can leisurely discuss the latest read-aloud over breakfast or toothbrushing, or who can tie it in neatly to an outing (we've seen any number of "prototypes" of Mike Mulligan's *Maryanne* out rusting away). And I think what a joke it was to imagine that I, as a teacher, actually knew any of the children I taught. Compared to what I know about my own children, I knew nothing about the kids who came to my classroom. Their backgrounds and home lives were blanks to me. I didn't know where they'd been, what they'd read, what they wondered about. How different to know a child intimately, my own child.

Publishing *Pennsylvania Homeschoolers* has broadened our family so much. We've certainly gained every bit as much as we've given out, and more. When I think of the pallid, complaining conversations of the smoky teacher's lounge at school, and compare them to the friendly, open, in-depth conversations and letters with homeschooling parents we've become close friends with, there is just no comparison. And our kids have friends through this wonderful homeschooling network that's formed in the past ten years. We've been with families that open up whole new worlds to us -- the ballet, owner built homes, piano, science projects we'd never thought of, sculpting with old apple logs, growing orchards of dwarf trees.

So I look about me and think of ten years of changes and how good it's been. I've seen Jesse grow from a toddler pointing chubby fingers at pictures of cows to a competent reader who finishes a book in two days because he just can't put it down. Jacob is almost 7 and always experimenting, concocting new "mixtures" and inventions and discussing air pressure and vacuums and trying to read all the signs he sees around him (this, a child who I know the schools might have quickly labeled LD). And Molly, now four, is writing stories daily, absolutely fearless about putting thoughts into print, and drawing astonishing pictures all the time. And now baby Hannah is here too, and we are all watching her with delight as she invents Bronx cheers and chortles away to us in baby jabber (the "whole conversation" approach to talking, I call it!). I remember once writing in a journal, when Jesse was about 18 months old, about how exciting it was to show him the birds that came to our feeder. I wondered what good things we'd be learning when he was 4. It's gone on long beyond that now, and it's still very exciting.

### Howard's Background

I met Susan when we were both in college taking courses in teacher education. After we graduated and got married, Susan worked at her first career, as a teacher in a Catholic school, while I went back to graduate school to get a Masters Degree in reading instruction. This degree helped me to get a job teaching reading in a public school, and when Jesse was born, Susan began her second career, this time as a mother.

I remember when Susan first began to mention homeschooling. I opposed the idea at first thinking that such a decision might put us into conflict with my school district and might cost me my job. I asked Susan why she couldn't do homeschooling activities with our children after they would come home from school. She showed me an article in *Growing Without Schooling* about a mother who had tried, but whose children came home from school too burned-out to do anything resembling school work. Finally, I gave my consent to homeschooling, a decision that I have never regretted.

Even if our children were not growing up to be literate, even if they were not growing up to be kind people, I would appreciate homeschooling because it has helped us be a close family. Also, many children in schools find that they have to choose between their peer group's values and their parents' values. Some choose their peer group's values and become strangers to their parents. I do not think that our children will ever be strangers to us.

Also, our decision did not cost me my job. We were able to make a cooperative agreement with our school district, and now I am not so much different from the many public school teachers who send their children to private schools.

When I was fifteen I once met my father at his job. He was a college professor and I attended the last ten minutes of one of his classes. I felt that there was a nice respectful atmosphere in that room and I decided then and there that I, too, would become a college professor. So, as I continued to teach during the day, I began to take night courses at the University of Pittsburgh working toward the doctorate in education which I obtained a few years ago.

My doctoral dissertation applied an artificial-intelligence program to the understanding of children learning sight words. Since completing my doctoral work I have been engaged in an extensive exploration of the artificial intelligence literature and hands-on programming of artificial-intelligence models on my home computer. I am now engaged in testing a program that I have just written which learns phonics. Through this work I hope to come to a better understanding of how children learn. Despite the many successful school reading methods, no one really knows how children learn phonics, and, certainly, no one knows how some three and four year olds teach themselves.

As a reading "expert," parents often come to me with questions about how they should teach reading at home. At first, I didn't know what to tell them. I knew many methods that work in schools but did not know whether they would be suited to the home, so I began to interview parents and children in order to find out how reading is learned at home. If there is a pattern it is this: The child begins his first steps into reading when he is being read to. He may be sitting on his mother's lap, or closely snuggled next to his mother. When he first begins reading himself, he is often in the same position. Whenever he needs help, his mother is there to help him and give him security. Later, he is sitting next to his mother, perhaps on a couch, and he is getting much less help. When he can't get a word he points to it and she helps him. Soon, he is reading at the kitchen table, while she is preparing supper. When he can't figure out a word he spells it out loud for her. Eventually, he is off by himself silently reading a book of many chapters.

Even after he has learned to read, he still snuggles with his brothers and sisters as his parents read aloud, sharing literature, math, history, and science, and family togetherness.

This Book

Chapters two, three, four, and five are about children's reading. They are arranged chronologically, beginning from when children first begin to listen to books that are read to them, and moving until they begin to read fluently to themselves. Chapters six, seven, and eight describe some of the informal and formal ways our children have learned writing and arithmetic. Chapters nine, ten, and eleven discuss some of the structures of homeschooling including achievement tests, curriculums, and the structure of the homeschooling day. Chapter twelve summarizes what we have learned about what works within our home.

# 2. Reading to Children

There is no audience more delightful to read for then homeschooled children. Our children chuckle out loud with delight at humorous passages in books that I read with them, and we just naturally stop and talk along the way, making remarks about the pictures or the story.

I have read several biographies of home educated children -- Thomas Edison, George Patton, Woodrow Wilson -- and I have always been struck by how important their early experiences of being read to were to them. Thomas Edison liked to hear his mother read biographies of famous scientists and he became one of the most famous. General Patton liked to hear war stories like the Iliad. There is even a story that he once dragged his sister around in a game where he was Achilles who had just slain Hector of Troy. He went on to become a great General in World War II. Woodrow Wilson's father, who was a Presbyterian minister with a love for the well put phrase, used to read Woodrow great speeches and together they would analyze the speaker's choice of words. Woodrow, himself, became a great speaker who could capture the ideals of the nation in his words. His "Fourteen Points" speech during World War I captured the imagination and the world and helped lead to an early end of the fighting and a negotiated peace.

I have met very few parents of home-educated children who do not read to their children on a regular basis beginning when their first child was a baby. I think that one of the main reasons that homeschooled children are generally such good listeners is because they have been read to and they have responded to stories all of their lives. This contact with books also leads them to have the vocabulary and background that enable them to understand and enjoy books when they do read to themselves.

Before I began to investigate home instruction, I supposed that parents would quit reading to their children once the children were able to read to themselves. I have been fascinated to find that reading continues with older children, because reading together is one of the best ways to share explorations of history, literature, science, religion and mathematics.

## Reading With a Baby

Our kids begin to listen to books when they are just babies. When Jesse was five and Jacob was just two, Susan wrote...

I remember wondering, while pregnant with my second child, how I'd ever be able to read to my older Jesse with a new baby around. I figured the early few months *might* go all right, as I could read while nursing the baby, but I really worried about what would happen as our little one began grabbing books from us -- would he eat or rip them, or generally make a muddle of our good sharing times? Would they be too far apart in age to ever enjoy the same stories at the same time?

I've been delighted with what's actually happened. The early months *were* very easy for reading aloud to Jesse. We'd all snuggle in bed together with a book, lots of nursing, and we'd all feel relaxed. I think my "reading voice" was lulling to Jacob in the same way as a crooning, singing voice: I was often amazed to find both boys would drift off to sleep at the same time after our readings.

As Jacob grew, he began to open his eyes a bit as I'd read, pupils dilating with delight while Jesse and I would laugh over some delicious passage. Jacob began laughing with us over favorite parts just to share in our fun, began peeking away from the breast to see the pictures, began patting pages. We weren't reading *to* him, or *for* him, we weren't trying to give our baby a "boost" in reading ability by "exposing" him to print at a properly early age. It's just that as a part of our family, Jacob was always *there*, and took part as best he could at every stage. He did at times make very loud noises while we read, he did sometimes throw our books on the floor, and he maybe gnawed on one or two, but generally, that just meant the timing was wrong, not that Jacob was destroying our reading time.

Jesse and I enjoyed together seeing Jacob begin to embrace books as his own. By a year, he'd fallen in love with *Goodnight Moon*, laughing as we'd touch the "hot" fire, pointing ecstatically to the real moon outside. We somehow passed over most of the cardboard baby books -- Jacob seemed to be catching on so quickly to gentle handling of books since they were always about EVERYWHERE, and obviously treasured. He also seemed to prefer real *stories* to mere "point it out" books. We found our reading choices move towards Jacob's new favorites -- we must have read and poured over *Angus* and *Ask Mr. Bear* books by Marjorie Flack a thousand times the month Jacob was fifteen months old. It was our delight to rediscover Jesse's old treasures and share them anew with Jacob. Jesse seemed to enjoy these simplest tales immensely, too, even though he was a "bigger boy" of four and a half and also listening to Rudyard Kipling's *Just So Stories* and *The Velveteen Rabbit* and *The Little House in the Big Woods* and other longer books. It wasn't a boring experience for him to hear the *Three Billy Goats Gruff* a hundred times -- he loved acting it out with his little brother, and also would see these timeless stories from his new older perspective, saw ever new questions to raise about them. I remember Jesse musing, "Well, I think they should have sent the *big* Billy Goat Gruff over the bridge *first*, then the littlest one wouldn't have had to be so scared by the troll, the big one could have gotten rid of that troll right away." I realized many times that we might never have gotten these first books off the shelf again if it hadn't been for Jacob growing into them and, so, bringing them back to *all* of us. Jesse also began to have Jacob's favorites learned by heart. I remember him at four and a half "reading" all of the *Little Fur Family* by Margaret Wise Brown to Jacob, with engaging inflection and proper pauses to ask Jacob little questions.

Sometimes we let special reading to Jacob slide and focus more on Jesse's books.  Jacob is used to falling asleep nursing while I read aloud, but again he always amazes us by popping in with appropriate comments or laughs when we think he's dozing. Jacob usually seems to grasp the main characters of our books, and so can follow and participate in Jesse's play-acting versions (*everything* seems to get acted out in our house!!!).  Shared stories have become a cement to their friendship, a vehicle for them to enjoy play together, as they both know and love the common themes of the stories woven through their days.  They share worlds through our books.  The years ahead look exciting and rich, and now we're wondering how next summer's baby-to-be (Molly) will enjoy it all.

### Reading to Answer Questions

**At home, reading together can be a way to explore just about just about every area of the curriculum.  These explorations often begin with the children's questions.**

Think over your day with your child at home...  How many times did your child come up with a thoughtful question, a sincere wondering, a puzzling observation?  Count yourself lucky if the question count was high, for this is a treasure reserved especially for homeschoolers.  This evening, reading a back issue of *Instructor Magazine* (October, 1968), I came across an article called, "Do Teachers Talk Too Much?"  Author William Floyd reports on his research into classroom teacher's questioning styles, and also student's opportunities to raise their own questions.  On average, in the 40 primary grade classrooms observed (recommended as BEST by their principals), he found that the teachers asked 96% of the questions, and the students only 4%. And this mere 4% was of course divided between whole classrooms of children, meaning that most never asked any questions at all. The record breaking teacher fired out 283 questions in one hour -- while her students asked not one at all. Overall, each child's question was balanced out by an average of 27 questions by the teacher. This lop-sided chance to question is bad enough, but the nature of the pupils' questions is probably most disturbing. Floyd writes that it perhaps wasn't surprising that the questions the school children DID ask showed almost no thought or real interest. The kids were merely checking up on what the teacher had said, or were asking for permission to speak. Floyd found there was basically neither time nor opportunity for the children to really raise questions -- sincere, thought-provoking questions from the students were clearly not part of the teachers' expectations. The teachers held the floor, and the kids were there to answer, not question.

Floyd concludes, with real sadness, that the children not only did not have much idea of how to ask good questions, they did not have any idea that wondering and asking about their world might even be an important or appropriate job for them.

Reading this article made me think of the many and varied questions Jesse and Jacob ask in a day, and the many chances we all have for leisurely discussion and sharing -- and how lucky I feel! In just the past several days I've begun to jot down some of their questions. Here's a sampling:

- How do frogs get air when they're hibernating in the mud under a pond?

- Why are poodles often chosen for circus dogs?

- What letters make the sound "aw?"

- Guess what? Do you know what the notes in an F chord are?

- Where does cinnamon come from?

- What is this fort a picture of? (Fort McHenry? I

thought so!!!)

• What are apostrophes for?

• Why did people used to like beaver furs so much?

• Was the new territory that the English won from the French during the French and Indian War, was it considered one of the colonies that broke away from England in the Revolution?

• How big a city is Chicago?

• Why don't the little countries all around Israel just make peace with Israel?

• Why did they make Washington D.C. a city all by itself, not part of any state?

• Why doesn't wolverine fur freeze?

• Why did they have that lexan shield above the dinosaurs in the museum?

Often these questions come up at meandering, quiet times of the day -- if Jesse is hanging about the kitchen as I fix a meal, while we're on a long car ride, or after Jesse has been balancing on his head on a stuffed chair. Odd moments, unplanned moments. They usually spur a whole little discussion, always making me see the issue in question in a new way, making me realize that as a "sophisticated" adult I'd never thought the problem through before, never even knew there was a question there. Often we turn to reference books or maps about the house to further explore an issue. (The question about Chicago got us using an almanac for the first time, and we ended up comparing Chicago to Pittsburgh to the state of Alaska, comparing populations in two different censuses, as well as surface area.)

I think it's very safe to say that these questions would never have been asked by Jesse at a school. There would have been no time, no "permission," no expectation and welcoming of questioning. No one to listen and ponder and toss the questions around with. It often isn't so necessary to answer their questions, as it is to *value* their questions, show interest in their emerging ideas. Because they've raised a question, it shows they've already been doing serious thought about the issue, already may have some hunches or theories of their own, and so I often ask what they've thought so far. They aren't seeking "information" from an "expert," so much as wanting a colleague to discuss their path of thought.

You might want to think back to your own schooling days, and see how many opportunities you had to raise questions and share them with a responsive adult. If your children are now in school, you might want to do an unobtrusive "question count" in your child's classroom and see if Floyd's 1968 findings are still valid today (I'd be willing to wager they are). You might want to try to write down some of your child's questions for a day or two -- you'll probably be surprised to find just how many opportunities our home-taught children have to comfortably inquire and wonder about all of the world.

And should we "count" the times when our children pose questions as official "instructional time," part of our "5 hours per day, 180 days a year?" You bet we should. It is, after all, probably one of the most powerful learning tools we are giving our children -- the confidence to raise their own questions.

**The rest of this chapter consists of Susan's articles about how reading aloud has been involved in our study of almost every subject area.**

## Science in Your Neighborhood

As we travel about Pennsylvania, we keep being amazed at how many fascinating places our state holds for kids and parents to visit.

When I was an elementary school teacher, "field trips" were usually just an interruption or an amusement to make the last weeks of the school year tolerable. They rarely seemed to be broadening or indepth experiences. Nothing was followed through on back in the classroom, and there was no time for a teacher to hear any wondering questions raised by students, if any questions were in fact raised during these "mob" outings.

How different it is to go somewhere as a family! *The Drake Oil Well Museum Memorial Park*, Titusville, is one favorite spot of ours. This is the site where the very first oil well in the world was drilled. Sometime after our first visit there, we found the children's biography, *Drake Drills for Oil*, which helped us to understand the man, Drake, and the great difficulties he faced trying to find a way to get oil from the ground in large quantities in 1860. For our second visit this summer (Molly was ten days old and slept through it all in her "sling pouch" carrier!), we borrowed the book again and read it on the drive to Titusville. The large museum at the park is run by the Pennsylvania Historic Sites and Museum Commission, and houses historical dioramas, displays of artifacts on the history of lighting, models of oil rigs of different eras, old photographs, and much more. There is also an auditorium showing a film about Drake and his discovery (made an interesting comparison to the book we'd just read). On the grounds the original derrick has been reconstructed, with an old steam engine to run the drill. There is also a cannon at the museum, used to blow holes in the bottoms of the wooden oil barrels in case of fire -- the oil could then drain out, leaving nothing to burn. My cannon-loving boys found this a good "peaceful" use for the weapon! If you visit the site in the summer months, you'll hear the wonderful clanging, squeaking, puff puffing and booms of an old gasoline powered oil rig, connected by an improbable spider network of cables to perhaps a dozen wells, all of it jerking and squeaking to the old motor's rhythms. Fascinating to watch!

We now notice all the old oil rigs dotting Pennsylvania roadsides, know where the kerosene for our lanterns comes from, as well as the gasoline for our cars, know a bit more about how an important discovery right here in our own state changed history. We have another "notch" to hang other dates on -- "Oh! the Civil War started right when Drake was scraping for oil from the creek!" or "See, Laura and Mary's family could have had kerosene for their lamps out on the prairie cause that was *after*

Drake." The drive to Titusville takes you by all the modern
Pennzoil refineries, bringing you right up to the 20th century.

And of course when we got home from the outing, Jesse and
Jacob acted out the whole story with blocks and wooden toys...

For years now we've driven by a sign in *Tarentum* (on our
way to Pittsburgh) saying *Tour-Ed Coal Mine -- 1 mile.* This
summer we finally made time to stop in (it was on the way to a
prenatal midwife visit -- Molly will have to wait a year to see
it!). We already knew something of coal, as the hill on our farm
had been stripmined thirty years ago and new stripmines are
always being opened in our county. Our neighbor, also, worked
in a deep mine. Coal also held a special interest for my boys as
they knew how important it was for running the steam engine
trains they love.

At Tour-Ed mine you can actually go into a mine on a small
electric "man-trip car." After a half mile trip into absolute
darkness, we all got out to see working displays of deep mining
methods, from hand pick and drill to the new rumbling, high-
powered continuous miners. Jesse's favorite part was being able
to use a pick-axe to hack out a piece of coal for himself. When I
told him that often children had worked in the early coal mines, I
could see the imaginings spinning through his head -- he threw
himself into the work with great concentration and gusto! Tour-
Ed also has life-size set-ups of an old miner's village, and a
demonstration strip mine, as well as picnic areas.

As we drove away, we talked long about why coal miners
were laid off right now, how coal relates to the steel and auto
industries, why children had worked in mines and how child
labor laws came about. Once home, we began listening to all the
coal-related folksongs in our record collection, and now know
the "Spring Hill Mine Disaster" by heart, even understanding all
the references to the "cutter blade" and the "rattle of the belt."
That week there were two severe explosions in deep mines,
killing a number of miners -- Jesse followed the news reports
with an understanding he couldn't have had before our trip. We
looked for children's books on coal at our public library, and

were able to borrow three excellent ones on inter-library loan
(one written by Isaac Assimov!).  We read them all, extending
our knowledge of the "black rock that burns."  We began noticing
coal references everywhere -- in the Laura Ingalls Wilder books,
in our train history books, in dinosaur books.  Jesse even began
discovering bits of coal in a "seam" of our unpaved driveway!
We touched the huge anthracite coal chunk at the Carnegie
Museum in Pittsburgh and began looking into the differences
between hard and soft coal.  (Unfortunately, the guide at Tour-
Ed was not at all helpful or respectful when Jesse asked *him*
about hard and soft coal -- he patted Jesse on the head
paternalistically and said one type was softer and then scooted
Jesse over to a mechanical horse for a free ride.  A proper
occupation for a child, better than asking questions.  Books were
a better resource, here, than a real person.)

**Everything Has a Story**
    Jesse and Jacob have always had a love of transportation
history -- we've read all about the history of railroads, canals,
ships, a bit about rockets, so I'm sure the automobile is on the
horizon.  I have also been surprised over the years how our on-
going reading in transportation history always DOES take us to
the important, but often too emphasized, OTHER subjects of
history -- the wars, the rulers, the political struggles and changes.
    We began a first interest in the Civil War times (an in depth
study this winter for all of us) through our train books -- had
found out the Civil War was the first war that used rail travel,
and this alone made it a very different type of war in many
ways...
    Reading about the building of the Erie Canal brought us to
understand how emigrants were treated in our country in those
times (they were given the back-breaking work that no "soft"
American would take...), and also helped us understand the
opening up of the West, the importance of trade routes, the way
cities sometimes are built up (New York boomed with the
Canal).  In short, it all has made me realize again what John Holt
said so often, that there is almost nothing in the whole world that

is unconnected to the rest of the drama of history. Not only does everything have a story, a history to it, but all these histories connect and overlap and tie-in with each other. There is always another question waiting, another investigation, and so many good books and resources to look to.

My boys have thoroughly incorporated the habit of asking the "story" questions about anything new they come upon -- we've looked into the history of bread, paper, printing, fabrics, paintings, music, coal, oil, astronomy, calendars, even VELCRO, finding good stories everywhere, and finding that no matter how diverse our reading goes, it all ties in with what we already know. I remember one time, reading about the history of BREAD, when we came across a story about CRESCENT rolls being invented in Austria by a baker who had understood and averted a Turkish plan to overtake Vienna (the crescent was a symbol of Turkey). We happened to read this right after attending a concert with a Mozart piece that had used Turkish instruments (including a CRESCENT shaped clanging shaking rhythm instrument) in the opening, because everyone was a bit wild for Turkish music then, after the Turkish invasions! We are hardly astonished by such serendipity anymore, but take it as the normal (and delightful!) course of events in the world.

## Electricity Explorations

Today Jesse astounded me. He is 6 1/2 years old and today he rewired two lamps (one never functional before) and figured out and made a needed minor repair on a third. I was essentially off taking a bath with the two littler ones. I didn't really want to get involved with all this wire-stripping work as my mind was on the house cleaning necessary for a pending visit from friends. My attitude was, "Oh, yeah, well maybe, Jesse, just let me vacuum, do the dishes, wash diapers, mop, do the bathroom and bake bread and make soup for supper and if there's any time left, sure I'll help you do the electricity work." But Jesse had PLANS, he was ready, he was twitching to get at these lamps, pull their wires out and go to it. "Well, what's the first thing I need to do?" he pestered. I relented a bit, looked it over with him a

moment, Molly on my hip. The way was pointed and he was off.
Jesse has a fine understanding of electricity gained from a year
and a half of wide ranging experimenting and work with it --
from homemade battery testers, to repairing flashlights, to
making electromagnets, to wiring up tinker toy inventions, to
gouging apart dry cells to see the insides, to pulling apart broken
electric meat grinders, clocks, record players and radios, to
racing about shaking strings of beads with Jacob pretending to be
electrons.

Back to the lamps -- I was still in the tub when Jesse brought
in the first completed lamp. The big moment had come -- the
new bulb carefully screwed in, plug inserted in socket. Click.
And -- an amazement to us all -- LIGHT!!! (Note -- we don't
recommend mixing electricity with bathtubs -- we happen to
have a very large bathroom, and Jesse was nowhere near the
tub...) Jesse had done every step himself -- pulling out the old
cord, scrounging a new one (recycled from an old blender and
saved by Jesse, he'd KNOWN it would come in handy!),
stripping the wires, wrapping and screwing them onto the light
socket posts, putting everything back in place, climbing to a high
shelf to get new bulbs...

Perhaps I'm most amazed at this morning's work because I
come from such an UN-handy about the house family. Minor
repairs ALWAYS meant hiring professionals. I never once saw
anyone in my family even attempt to wire a lamp -- the idea of
being able to delve into a lamps "innards" wouldn't have even
occurred to us. At school I likewise learned nothing of these
practical arts of simple home repairs -- science classes were
mostly non-existent when I was Jesse's age and by junior high
we were immediately plunged into the periodic table of elements
and balancing chemical equations. (Did teachers assume we all
had practical backgrounds to make these ideas real?)

And so I see now several more values to homeschooling --
it's given us working lamps for our livingroom, and a young boy
who feels just pride in real and helpful work responsibly done.
Homeschooling has helped ME follow my son's lead and learn

by his side.  Jesse and I surely would not have learned about rewiring lamps if a year and a half ago we hadn't begun scrounging for simple books on electricity, begun actual experiments with static, bulbs, batteries, wires, and magnets.  It was these simple experiments which gave ME the courage to rewire MY first lamp a year ago.  It is never too late to learn...

I think sometimes parents who feel disheartened to read about home-schooled kids doing all sorts of wonderful things "all on their own" may really be asking to know how the whole interest came about.  They may just want to know the PROCESS of how the kid got to the point where he could do some astonishing thing "all on his own."  And I think in most cases there IS a long process behind good accomplishments.  Maybe parents just can't find it helpful to hear only about end PRODUCTS.  What we really want to know is the first inklings of interest, the slow beginnings, the amount of time and growing that a final accomplishment embodies.  For me to tell people that Jesse can wire up speakers on his own, or rewire lamps, doesn't really mean anything unless they know the context of his learning, a context that in our case certainly involved ME a lot.

I was involved not so much as teacher (I knew little more about electricity than Jesse did in the beginning), but instead as a colleague.  We were JOINTLY interested in all our electricity work, and our interest got Howard involved also, and HE took the work much farther than Jesse or I would've on our own.  Jesse didn't just "all on his own" come up with a whole agenda of things he wanted to do with electricity and set about doing them with no input from us.  As he wasn't reading during our first electricity binge I was the vehicle for him to gather new information about the subject.  I found the books, I read them aloud, I mused aloud about parts I didn't understand, I took him to the hardware store for a special trip to buy needed supplies, I was ready to help him set up experiments that would have been too hard for him to do on his own, I was excited about our growing knowledge and understanding.

Now, if Jesse suddenly began playing expert baseball (he still calls footballs baseballs and vice versa, sports not being a big interest of our family), or spinning figure eights on the ice (we do have a farm pond that is probably perfect for skating but I haven't set skate blade to it in 10 years, not liking to get my feet cold in winter), or if he suddenly began playing tuba or riding horses or any number of things that we just don't do (yet) -- well, that would be magic and I'd be as astonished as anyone. But his electricity work and play has a long history to it and has just gradually grown and grown.

Just one more note about electricity and a free source of great wire to experiment with. Check your local phone company and ask them for some pieces of wire that they are throwing away. If brave, ask if you can peek in their dumpster. The kids and I were astonished to see 5 huge bins FULL of wire and cables and occasional parts of old phones and connectors and switches. I at first thought the wire would probably be sent on to a recycler -- all that COPPER -- but we were told that, no, it was all to be thrown out. We gratefully packed our little car to the brim. The bright colored very flexible wire encased in larger cables is also great fun to make wire sculpture and wild jewelry and gizmos and what-nots. And it's just as good as what stores sell (rather expensively) as "bell wire" for simple battery experiments. We also got ROLLS and rolls of heavier black wire (it is what Jesse used to string up his speakers), and all in all just felt like we had run into TREASURE. Maybe a homeschooling group could plan a tour through a telephone company, and ask in advance if the kids could all have some wire afterwards.

### The Soldier Game

Jesse and Jacob have never been involved at all with super heroes or He-men. We have no TV, don't go to toy stores much, and are usually simply blithely unaware of all these commercially pushed fantasies. The boys somehow agree with me that all those muscled toy dolls are hideous and creepy. For me, perhaps, the commercial, adult, pre-made fantasy aspects are what distress me the most about this sort of play -- it is adult made specifically for children, with no referents in the real continuum of human experience. I wonder if this sort of play can go anywhere, evolve into something personally meaningful, help the child to make sense of the real world.

Jesse and Jacob *have* evolved over four years time, though, an elaborate war-play game, and I'd like to share some of that with you now. As a new mother strange to the ways of little boys play, I often worried about how I'd handle the GUN Question. I had an older sister, and though I fancied myself something of a tomboy, war play was not one of my interests, ever. In college, I'd seen an alternative pre-school refuse to allow gun play, only to see the little boys push the rule to its limits by trying torpedoes, cannons, bombs, etc. The exasperated, but somewhat amused teachers finally felt that perhaps it was just not a possible rule to fully maintain, but that at least they'd put a bit of a damper on violent weapon play. I probably hoped my sons would simply not be at all interested in this type of play. Not so.

Jesse's first war interests came at about 3 1/2, when we visited Fort Frederica, a National Historical Site in Georgia near where my mother lives. We saw a filmed re-enactment of the fort and town settlement, we walked all about the excavation sites, and Jesse, of course, climbed on the cannons. It was love at first sight, those cannons. The place had a good story to it, and Jesse was hooked. Interesting, though, that *I'd* never found the place at all interesting when my family moved to the area when I was entering college, my "blase days" when little in the real world held much interest. I'd yawned my way through the site a few perfunctory times back then, but really found it utterly boring. Now, through Jesse's questioning eyes, the site became alive for us all. It was perhaps a first experience for Jesse in realizing that life was not always the present day, that there indeed was something called a past history, some dimly perceived continuum. Why, you could even dig it up!

Back at Grandma's house he spent hours delightedly acting out the battle scene with the Spanish forces from Florida attacking the undermanned English fort. He would sneak into the livingroom quietly, I would have to be the "lookout" at Fort Frederica and spy him out, and then the battle would ensue. Replayed again and again.

My mother was a bit surprised when the next year on our vacation visit, we wanted to go to the fort again, for after all we had "done" it the year before and would surely be bored by a repeat. Not so. We sat through the movie several times, remembering parts we'd seen before, putting together more historical pieces. That time, we read aloud all the exhibit signs, looked more carefully and thoughtfully at the miniature dioramas, felt more keenly the spirit of life in the now utterly gone town. More acting out of the battles, that year with closer attention to details we now understood better. Jesse received a huge set of cardboard brick blocks from Grandma, and they were used to build myriad forts and invading fleets of boats. Postcards of old soldiers were bought at the Fort, and a miniature cannon (!), and again the play went on for hours. Jesse also worked hard making some collage soldiers for extras, while Jacob at 18 months did his best to take part, probably feeling that this soldier game was the best sort of hide and seek and chase game there was.

Each year we returned to the fort, each year we loved it even more. Books extended our understanding, and I even found myself looking into a few adult history books on the area.

Other war interest grew over those years, too, and continued broadening our view and the boys' play. Any cannon was spotted and visited if at all possible, and we soon found ourselves at the Soldiers and Sailors Civil War memorial in Pittsburgh, Gettysburg, Fort Pitt, Fort Necessity, The Flagship Niagara, Fort Ligonier (with a homeschoolers group tour last fall), and another fort site in Georgia. A timeline gradually began forming in our minds: Ft. Frederica before Ft. Necessity, Ft. Necessity before Ft. Pitt, Civil War much later (we always peg *it* by Drake's discovery of oil). Our reading aloud, in among *Peter Pan* and *Heidi* and *The Wizard of Oz*, was full with history. Each fall we always read several biographies of Columbus (special interest of mine as I was born on Columbus Day), adding one a year, then the same with the Pilgrims in November. We found a book on the history of forts in America, archaeology in Georgia, Pennsylvania history, a Lois Lenski book called *Indian Captive* (based on the real life story of Mary Jamison, who decided to remain with the Senecas after her capture during the French and Indian Wars). We read about Jamestown and Pochahontas, we read biographies on many early American leaders (especially love the D'Aulaires biographies on Columbus, Franklin, Lincoln, Leif Ericson, and George Washington, and Jean Fritz's simple and wonderful Revolutionary War books -- *And Then What Happened, Paul Revere?*, *What's the Big Idea, Ben Franklin*, *Why Don't You Get a Horse, Sam Adams*, *Where was Patrick Henry on the 29th of May*, *Can't You Make Them Behave, King George?*). Forts led into an interest in war ships, and we've read extensively about the USS Constitution and many others. Connections were forming, a web of interrelated drama was being forged. Also, to offset war as the sole way of looking at history, we've also read all the Little House books by Laura Ingalls Wilder, and *Caddie Woodlawn* by Carol R. Brink (feeling through it of course the underlying pulse of the Civil War taking place far away), and we've read about the history of transportation, especially trains and canals and ships.

Jesse and Jacob gradually added more cannons to their play, made their block forts both more elaborate and more true to the forts they knew about, made fleets and fleets of paper and cardboard boats (anyone want to go in on a case-load order of masking tape???). Actual battles were often acted out, with lots of loud "bang-banging" filling the air. This was their "soldier game," and they were always begging Howard to take part. They knew I was rather dull about it and not much into their re-enactments, much as I loved visiting the actual sites and reading to them about these older times. Somehow I just cannot get into being down on hands and knees and "banging" away and the boys have eventually accepted this. Jesse and Jacob have

spent long happy stretches of time cutting out "armies" of men --
hundreds of different colored strips of paper bundled together
with rubber bands by 10's and 100's, complete with generals and
captains.  They lay them out in elaborate battle formations and
become enraged if I inadvertently sweep up or try to toss out a
crumpled regiment.  The soldiers are kept in special boxes,
stored with aluminum foil carefully rolled into cannon balls.

On occasion I've thought of discouraging all this play,
considering the GUN Question, feeling disheartened that my
boys saw wars as such a game, such an exciting play theme, such
an abstraction of paper soldier deaths.  I'm glad now I've let it be
and let it evolve and grow.  It is their play, it belongs to them,
and further it is clearly becoming their way of grappling with all
the real questions of how people have and might get along in this
world.  Besides banging wildly, they've also worked hard at
making peace treaties -- Daddy's soldiers will get all of the
living room, Jacob's will have the attic and Jesse's will patrol the
connecting zone of the playroom.  They've made compromises,
seen what happens when one side secretly doesn't go along with
an agreement, they've made allies and promises of future aid.

And, then, just yesterday, I sat in the attic nursing Molly to
sleep while Jesse and Jacob continued their new version of the
soldier game.    Both rebuilt elaborate block forts, sturdily
reinforced, the paper ship fleets were lovingly repaired with
masking tape, all was set. BUT THE BATTLE DIDN'T COME.
Jesse looked up at me after a silence (I was reading a magazine),
and said very quietly, almost reverently, "Look, look at this
small building I've made... It is the House of Peace... It has one
soldier in it, with NO weapons allowed, and it is where each side
can come, in safety, to talk." His voice was almost choked, full
with emotion.  He took a wooden sculpted head (a leftover from
an old tenant who was an artist of sorts), and placed it by the
little building.  "This is the grim-face of Peace, looking grimly at
all the war."  Another larger, grinning sculpture was placed by
the huge fort.  "This is the smiling face of War, it looks down
gleefully on all the fighting and destruction." We talked here of

how Ares, the war god we'd met in the D'Aulaires book of
Greek Myths always loved the battle scene. A metal crown (an
old bongo drum rim, I think) was placed on the War God's head,
as his side was winning over the much smaller God of Peace.
Jesse and Jacob were both hushed and serious, this was
important drama coming alive before them, universal questions
hanging in a delicate balance. I was careful not to intrude.
Somehow, over the next long half hour, Jesse and Jacob's armies
were secretly meeting at the Peace House, their generals talking
quietly and safely, and then -- TRIUMPH!!! PEACE won out!
Plans were swiftly made to join the two opposing forts together
in one large cooperative complex. Much reshuffling of blocks to
bridge the ground between them, much excitement over these
new plans. And when the rebuilding was complete, Jesse with
solemn ceremony took the crown from the War God's head and
placed it upon the Head of Peace, who somehow looked happier
to us all, not so grim-faced. The whole drama felt like a
refreshing cleansing, a noble setting of the world to right. We all
took deep breaths of peace, and went down for supper keenly
alive and aware, and *kind.*

If I had "banned" their soldier game out of some urge of my
own to have my boys be peaceful and peace-loving, this scene
could never have happened, they could never have grown to this
point. Their growing and play of course, did not take place in a
vacuum, but against the rich background of our reading and
continuing discussions. We just this week completed reading
Esther Forbes' Newberry Award winning book *Johnny Tremain*
set in pre-Revolutionary War Boston, culminating in the battle of
Lexington. The book moved Jesse perhaps more than any we
have ever read -- it's the first book I remember him crying aloud
over. It gave an especially close, sensitive look at the realities
and ambiguities of war, the mixed and torn feelings involved.
Johnny, an active young patriot, has warm feelings for many
specific British soldiers -- knowing them personally, having his
life entwined with theirs, it is hard to see them a abstract
"targets" of scarlet. Instead of taking us into the actual battle

scenes, Forbes has Johnny walk from Boston to Lexington the day after, seeing the crying women and children, the burial carts, the groaning wounded British soldiers, and finally the death of Johnny's beloved friend Rab.

I'm sure the soldier game will continue to grown and change as the years go by. The boys have already talked about having Molly be "Molly Pitcher" -- will be curious to see how Molly perhaps softens the game. I feel comfortable now about it all, rather than exasperated or guilty. I feel a trust that through their play they will all be made more ready to deal with the terribly difficult questions of war and peace in the real world. I feel hopeful when Jesse says, as he did today, that maybe a problem with these grown up real generals is that they still think they're playing with toy soldiers, and not real people.

## Civil War Times

Our studies of history and social studies have always grown organically, spiraling out from one core interest to weave into all our understandings. And so it's been with our study this winter of the Civil War times. When I think of the pallid bare bones information a school text book gives, I shudder. We've ranged far, finding resources everywhere.

We've read biographies together, beginning the whole study with four biographies of Lincoln. We always start out a study with the very simplest material we can find -- in this case the "Really Truly" series biography of Lincoln by the Lowitz's (a delightful series written in the 1930's). We moved up through the D'Aulaires, Genevieve Foster, and finally to the in-depth and poetic biography by James Daugherty (Carl Sandburg is waiting in the wings...). All through this we compared and contrasted these books -- noting where basic information was different, how each author chose to focus on some parts of Lincoln's life and leave other parts alone. Biography involves lots of DECISIONS, involves an AUTHOR not just a subject, and the boys really understand this. We understood more of Lincoln's life with each book, and by the end had a fair grasp of the course of the Civil War, too, and its strands of causes.

But we weren't done.   The boys knew little previously of slavery (surely a seamy, unsavory side of our history, one I hadn't been overly eager to bring up with them).   So now we went on to biographies of black Americans of the time -- Frederick Douglas, Harriet Tubman, George Washington Carver. We saw how many of these lives were twined in with ones we'd heard of in our Lincoln books.   We went on then to *Amos Fortune, Free Man*, and a biography of the black poet Phyllis Wheatley, and gained a view of slavery in NORTHERN cities in Revolutionary War times.   Quite a different picture from the South with its sprawling tobacco farms and overseers.   The reality of slave voyages, the practiced cruelty of the "pits," the determination to separate captured Africans from their tribesmen, were all brought before us and discussed.   We were gaining a background, a peopled backdrop for the Civil War issues.

But there was still more to read.   We went to the facsimile copies of Civil War newspapers I'd bought years ago from a homeschooling mother who had found them in a public school DUMPSTER!   (I've almost always found it pays to pick up interesting resources inexpensively when I come across them, even if we aren't about to use them anytime soon -- almost everything EVENTUALLY finds its time!)   The newspapers were astonishing, really giving us the feel of being present in those times (even looked over the "Want Ads" in the 1863 *New York Times*, and laughed over how many were for "reputable wet nurses" -- and realized that in the South there would not have been such ads because slave mothers would have been used).

We also began ranging beyond official children's resources, finding our growing background made us ready for more adult books.   We began leafing through a stack of old *American Heritage* magazines we'd picked up for a song at library book sales.   With Bruce Catton, well-known Civil War writer, as editor, the old copies we had were full of incredible Civil War articles.   A first person account of the hanging of John Brown. The report by a newspaper war correspondent of his three years following General Grant (the kid's history books never went into such detail about Grant's severe drinking problem...). The story of how Booker T. Washington was able to first rise above the abjectness of slavery conditions. The gripping saga of a slave ship rebellion in the 1840's. The memoirs of privates who'd fought in the first Battle of Bull Run. Our view of these times was being fleshed out, peopled with unforgettable characters. No question here of "memorizing" information and facts -- we were coming to KNOW these times, and every new discovery could be hinged right on to our growing framework.

Howard got involved in this study too. He has sometimes been a bit left out of in-depth work like this in the past, because we'd do all this while he was away, and because he hasn't always had a regular reading time with the kids. That changed with this work. He began checking out Civil War books that HE was interested in reading, and sharing them with the kids. He found some intriguing ones I never would have come across, including one with words to almost all the Civil War songs you can imagine.

Which brings me to music -- we found a great musical history resource that tied in with this study. It's *The LIFE History of the United States* published by TIME/LIFE in 1963, a 12 record set, probably available in most public libraries. One side of each record has a sampling of music from each time period in our country's history -- instrumental music, spirituals, work songs, folk songs, war rallies, and church music. The flip side has important documents and speeches of the day, including snatches from diaries, letters, and famous books and poems. The boys LOVED these records, and played them endlessly. They actually loved them BEFORE we began reading about these times, but they found that once they had more background and information they could appreciate them so much more. Often as I'd be reading aloud to the boys, they'd stop me to say, "Hey! Isn't that on our record!?!" and we'd get it out, play it, and listen with new understanding and interest.

The culmination of all of this work was presenting a display

at the Fullmer's spring SOCIAL STUDIES FAIR. At first we
wondered what "project" we could do, so we could have
something to share and show.  It then hit me that often times in
school the whole idea of "projects" is a bit backwards -- it's
hoped that by doing something nifty, MAKING something,
perhaps for a display, that this will MOTIVATE the kids to
WANT to do research on a topic.  In our case our project WAS
our research -- all the many hours of talking, reading, wondering,
making new connections -- and all the singing of "We are
Coming, Father Abraham" and "Marching through Georgia." We
didn't really need to do anything different now just to officially
have a "project." So we just set out a display of most of the
books we'd read, the records, the old newspapers, the magazines,
and Jesse talked (on and on) about what we had learned.  Jesse
did make a large poster with a few simple illustrations and the
title "ABE LINCOLN, SLAVERY, AND THE CIVIL WAR,"
and Jacob helped me make a poster listing all the books we'd
read in different categories.  The kids also decided to make Abe
Lincoln "stove pipe" hats, as we'd read so many funny stories of
how he'd used his hat to hold important mail, memos, and
reminders, and they all had great fun doing that.  Jesse then
decided that he'd have a facsimile copy of the Gettysburg
Address hidden in the hat when he talked about our exhibit at the
Fair.  This idea came from Jesse and Jacob, and they also had
full input into HOW the hats would be made, with a good bit of
trial and many "errors."  We weren't following a script here, or a
recipe, but finding our own way.  I thought we could also sing
with the group at the Fair one of the Civil War songs we'd really
enjoyed, "Goober Peas" (a song about peanuts, a staple food of
the Southern army, which they considered cow feed, since no
PEOPLE ever ate peanuts in those days -- peanut butter hadn't
yet been invented!).  The Fair gave ME the motivation to
actually sit down and listen to the record about 30 times until I
REALLY knew all the actual words to the song (I don't think I'll
ever forget them now...), and I got practicing on my guitar.  At
the Fair several mothers came up to me with further suggestions

of Civil War books to read, ones THEY had enjoyed with their kids. It was a very special sharing time.

After we felt we had about fulfilled our Civil War interest, I did happen to find we owned a fifth grade Scott Foresman 1979 Social Studies textbook (Jesse and Jacob were officially 3rd grade and kindergarten then), and it had a big "unit" on the Civil War. The book looked attractive enough, rather classy and colorful, not drab at all, and I thought it might have some further information and insight for us. What a stunning disappointment -- it was just the usual school tripe, just in a more pleasing format. Names were bandied about non-stop with no real description of the PEOPLE behind the names, and then the kids were of course "quizzed" on the names. One three sentence paragraph on Harriet Tubman. Three sentences about Frederick Douglas. One on Clara Barton. And SHORT sentences at that -- choppy things, carefully metered out in proper fifth grade lengths. I just cannot imagine any child using this text book coming to LOVE learning about these times, feeling a part of that life or feeling any reason to really integrate and remember any of it. Just quiz and test; do the little canned projects and move on to the next unit. There was never once a suggestion to the child reader that he might want to look in other resources or books for more information or insight -- perhaps the authors suspected rightly that it would be enough of a chore for the teacher to get them "through" this one book. And so I felt doubly good about our "organically grown," unplanned-in-advance work, after comparing it to the official school stuff expected of kids two to five years older than mine. WE all actually learned something!

## Home Economics

Amazingly enough, housework is seeming like less of a problem to me these days. Partly this is due to changes in my attitudes following reading *Side-tracked Home Executives* by Pam Young and Peggy Jones. Partly it's due to our growing repertoire of "cleanup games." It's becoming easier and easier to think these up on the spur of the moment, and certainly makes daily pickup chores pleasanter. In one new game, Jesse works in one room, and I work in another. We must both pickup and put away *something*, then we must guess what it is that the other person has put away. Involves a lot of going back and forth between rooms, but is good fun *and* gets two rooms neatened.

I sometimes ask Jesse to pick up, say, the spilled contents of the Lincoln Log can, adding that I'll time him to see how long it takes. A stop-watch is great for this. This approach usually gets much more cooperation than a stern command, and even helps Jesse gain a firm sense of the meanings of seconds and minutes. If a friend is over, they can work cooperatively to do the task. Always good to see kids scurrying about to *help* each other rather than to *beat* each other. Also it's surprising to all of us how *little* time these "put away" jobs take.

The game Jacob, our almost 3 year old, finds most delightful might be called the "Silly Mommy Nonsense Direction Game." I'll ask him to please put away the masking tape, IN THE REFRIGERATOR! He'll laugh at his silly mother who must not know any better. I'll look confused, then maybe say, "Hmmm, in the *washing machine*?" More indulgent laughs, and finally Jacob himself says, "Tape goes on the TAPE HOOK!!!" and runs to put it there. (We have LOTS of low-down hooks in our house -- saves rooting about in messy drawers.) Jacob's other favorite is when I pretend something very light weight is very *heavy* -- "Oh, Jacob, I couldn't let *you* put away this green marker, it's MUCH too heavy, *I* can barely lift it!" More belly laughs and Jacob races away with the marker, usually now even putting it in the right place.

I'm also realizing that for many things the kids are doing,

they really *don't* need me sitting right by them "helping." Today, when Jesse and Jacob built wonderful houses and people out of our "wild clay" from our stream, I got the dishes washed, the refrigerator and freezer tops cleaned off, scrubbed the stove, and the oven door, and even did my three minute bathroom cleanup. I was right near, as they were working at the kitchen table, and we were all talking together happily the whole time. They didn't feel left out or ignored because I hadn't dropped everything to just sit and watch *them* work. I could always easily see what they were making, could comment as I felt like it, and none of these little jobs of mine were the type that couldn't bear an interruption of a minute or two. Perhaps some homeschooling parents worry that there are only two types of time in a day -- time spent directly with a child, when *you* do nothing else, or time spent directly with household tasks when the child must be out of the way. Perhaps more blending of these times is a more realistic, fruitful approach. It seems to work best for us, anyway.

A children's book by Phyllis Krasilovsky, *The Man Who Didn't Wash His Dishes* has also helped us greatly. I remember reading in Holt's *Escape from Childhood*, that probably most young children simply don't have our adult perspective to see the consequences of not doing various jobs. He writes,

> When we take the garbage out, we know the reason: if we don't take it out, the kitchen will eventually be full of garbage. In our mind's eye we can see it there, we can almost smell it. In this sense we could be said to have a *more* active fantasy life than the children. The child has no such fantasy. We may ask him, "What do you think would happen if we didn't take out the garbage?" He has no idea. He thinks, I suppose, the sack of garbage would just sit there where it is, what's so bad about that?"[1]

The Krasilovsky book tells what happens to a man who decides, each night, that he's just *too* tired to do his dishes, and so keeps putting off the task day after day. Finally, he can barely get in the front door because of the dirty dishes stacked everywhere, and he's even eaten out of all his ashtrays, soap dishes, flower pots, and vases. The book ends with a rainstorm washing all the dishes clean in the back of the old man's pickup truck, and the man resolving that from then on, he would always wash his dishes immediately after eating. Both of my boys think the story is very funny, and now whenever they nag me to stop washing dishes to help them with something I'll say, "Oh no! You want me to be the little old *woman* who never washed *HER* dishes." That's usually enough to get them laughing and let *me* finish my job. We've transferred the idea to other tasks -- we imagine what the house would be like if I NEVER folded the laundry... the heaping piles on top of the dryer, the empty clothes drawers, the entire house stuffed to bursting with unfolded clothes... And all this delicious imagining *while* we're folding and carrying the clothes!

One more children's book that's helped us to cooperate better around the house is *Pelle's New Suit*, a charming Swedish picture book by Elsa Beskow about a little boy who asks all of his relatives and the town tailor to help him out in making a new suit of clothes from his own little lamb's wool. Each person always answers Pelle's requests for help by very politely saying, "Oh! that I will gladly do, if while I'm doing _____ for you, you will do _____ for me." Pelle hauls wood, weeds carrots, tends cows, watches his baby sister, and ends up with a completed suit ready to show to his lamb. Now when Jesse asks me to do something for him, and it really is something he can't do for himself, I'll answer in Pelle language, "Oh, I will gladly mend your bluejeans for *you*, if while I am doing it, you will kindly clear off the breakfast dishes for *me*." Jesse always catches the "literary reference" and is ready to do his part as I help him...

## Literary Appreciation

This fall we were delving into a whole "cache" of old school readers and Jesse (7), Jacob (4), and I had an amazing in depth discussion about schools, expectations for learning, biases of textbook writers, and more. It all began after a particularly startling find in one of the second grade basal readers that we were randomly flipping through. I saw an illustration of a red steam shovel, with an overalled man next to it, done in the rather pallid style of basal reader illustrations of the 1950's. There was a vague resemblance here to our old favorite story, Virginia Lee Burton's *Mike Mulligan*. We looked closer and found that, indeed, this WAS *Mike Mulligan*, only it was strangely altered, edited, re-drawn, watered-down, strained and pureed. What was left was a pablum version of the robust, rollicking original. Our boys were shocked, as was I, to find all the lilt and poetry carefully removed and made "sensible" and "direct" and EASY. All "hard" words like "Mrs. McGillicudy" and "town constable" were struck, replaced by "a lady" and "some people." Mary Ann and Mike Mulligan no longer "finished the first corner, neat and square," they merely "cut around the first side of the cellar." There were not just single word substitutions, which would have been bad enough, but wholesale reworkings of entire passages, added "explanations," and paragraph eradications. My boys and I pored over the two stories, real one and adaptation, noting every discrepancy. Jesse and Jacob both have a fine ear for good language and storytelling. They love metaphor, delicious twists of a phrase, rhythmic refrains chanting through a story. They love odd quaint names for characters and villages. They saw right off that this basal reader rendition had stripped all that they loved best about *Mike Mulligan*. I told them how the committees who put these types of books together felt the original was too complicated and hard for young children to read, and they didn't realize that if a child grows up hearing and loving these words, they aren't hard at all to read in print because the child expects to find them.

Jesse culminated our days and days of discussion by reading

aloud to Jacob and me the entire *real* book of *Mike Mulligan*. He had never read such a long or "hard" book before. He just began reading full books a bit over a half year ago, and mostly reads books like *Little Bear* or *Danny and the Dinosaur*, and others in the "I CAN READ" series from Harper and Row. Jesse felt proud and amazed to read this book through, needing only very occasional help (usually *not* on any "hard" words, either). He then went on to Burton's *Choo Choo, the Story of a Little Engine who Ran Away*, and her Caldecott award winner *The Little House*. Again, same result -- what might have been considered "hard" words by controlled vocabulary standards weren't so hard at all because Jesse knew what to expect.

We talked about how perhaps some teachers and parents might mistakenly think this adaptation travesty *was* the real version of *Mike Mulligan*, and applaud the basal reader for giving kids a real classic good story. After all, the table of contents just listed the story as *by* Virginia Burton -- we had to search the small print in the acknowledgements to find the words "adapted from." Closer inspection showed that almost all the other stories in the book that had authors listed were *also* adaptations. We wondered how many children were turned off to these authors because of reading such "basalized" versions. Interesting also to note that the teacher's manual makes no mention of there being another, better version of *Mike Mulligan* available in the school library, or any other books by Burton, in their "Enrichment Activities" suggestions for further "stories to enjoy." Research has shown, too, that most teachers do *not* use many suggestions for extra activities -- *unless* the suggestion involves handing out dittoed worksheets on "skills."[2]

# 3. First Steps Toward Reading

Patience is a most important quality for parents who are helping their children learn to read at home. Almost every method of reading instruction works if children are permitted to move at their own pace. Just as a child usually crawls before he walks and walks before he runs, he usually learns letters before words, and learns to read aloud before he begins to read silently.

A child is still learning letters if he finds it easier to read capital letters than lower case letters. He is still learning words if he finds it easier to read aloud than to read to himself. He is fluent when he reads long books to himself for his own enjoyment.

## Learning to Read in School

American schools used to begin teaching reading in first grade when children are six. (In Denmark, schools begin teaching reading when children are seven.) Now, American schools start teaching reading in kindergarten when children are just five. Talk to any sixty-year-old kindergarten teacher. She will tell you that kindergarten isn't the "child's garden" that it used to be. Now children sit at desks and study letters and letter sounds by filling in reams of "skill sheets."

Some children are ready to learn such things when they are five, others are not. Those who learn them go on to become good readers. Those who don't, go on to become poor readers and school failures. In one study, researchers found that those children who could not read letters quickly at the beginning of first grade, could not read words well at the end.[3] Another study has shown that the child who can't read well at the end of first grade, still can't read well at the end of sixth grade.[4]

Some children in kindergarten are just not as mature as other children. Not only do children grow up at different rates, but also some children are just barely five at the beginning of kindergarten, while others are five and a half or six. Joel Erion, a homeschooling father and school psychologist in Pennsylvania, looked at the birthdates of children who had been in school for many years but were doing so badly that they had been labeled as having "learning disabilities." He found that the average learning disabled child had been younger than the average normal child when he entered school. In other words, just because he was younger when he started school, he failed in school.[5]

More boys than girls fail in school and researchers have looked all over for explanations. Is it that female elementary school teachers are better at teaching girls? Is there a fundamental difference between boys' brains and girls' brains? I suspect that boys are just less mature than girls when they enter kindergarten, they aren't as good at talking and they are less ready to sit still and study letters.

At the end of kindergarten, children in schools take a "reading-readiness" test to determine if they are ready for first grade. Those who can't identify letters, or who don't seem to be able to concentrate, are sometimes held back.

In first grade, the class is generally divided into reading groups so that the better readers can progress quickly while the poorer readers may plod more slowly. Soon, the good readers believe that they are smart and the poor readers become imbued with the sense that they are dumb. Meanwhile, all the children are bored as they fill out endless phonics sheets. One word about phonics sheets: A recent study pointed out that phonics worksheets are used by teachers to keep children busy.[6]

Meanwhile, in the low reading group, the child who cannot easily identify the letters may manage to cope when there are only a few words on a page, but begins to get very frustrated when there are many unknown words on each page. He starts to fidget and looks anywhere in the room except at his books. If you ask him, he will tell you that he hates to read.

After first grade, the better readers continue to read the reading textbooks although they already know the words before they are presented, and the children in the low group continue to read the reading textbooks although the textbooks are frustratingly difficult. Some poor readers are held back in first grade for a second chance. When they are finally passed into second grade, they are still in the low group despite the extra year of reading instruction. They never choose to read on their own because they have come to hate reading. As they progress into junior high school and their school subjects involve more and more reading, many of them fail in other subjects. Because of flunking, they often enter high school two years later than their agemates. Many drop out of school, and many of these drop-outs later fill our prisons and welfare rolls.

## Learning to Read at Home

At home there is a completely different story. First of all, children learn to read at a much wider variety of ages. Some learn at three and others at twelve, and there are some who learn to read at every age in between.

I am presently following about twenty home-schooled children who did not begin to read until the age of seven or older, and thus far several of them have become fluent readers. I am guessing that all homeschooled children will eventually become fluent because they have been read to from birth and love books.

Children who learn to read at three or four seem to

become readers overnight, while children of eight or ten
appear to take two or three years to become readers. Is it
that little children have an easier time with reading? I think,
instead, that parents of three year olds judge their children's
abilities using a different yardstick than parents of six year
olds or parents of ten year olds. If a three year old can read
twenty words, he or she is a reader, but a six year old must
be able to read an easy-to-read book, and a ten year old must
be able to silently read a book with many chapters. A child
of any age can quickly learn to read ten or twenty words, but
it takes several months of effort before he can read an easy
book and several years before he can silently read a chapter-
book. So, in a sense, it takes a child longer to learn to read if
he is older just because he has to go so much farther before
he is considered a "success."

Dr. Raymond Moore points out that early reading can
lead to eye difficulties and prescriptions for glasses.[7] This is
especially true where the child is anxiously straining his eyes
to look at the words on a page. Sometimes reading glasses
are prescribed in order to decrease the eye strain of reading
small print. Such eye strain could also be decreased by
keeping reading times short, print big, and interposing
periods of relaxation where the eyes focus on objects far
away. Susan relates her own experience with eye strain...

I got reading glasses as a young teenager (13 years old, not an
easy time to begin wearing glasses!), and definitely found that I
once again began to love to read. The strain was off. Over the
past several years (or, I should say, whenever my glasses break
or get lost) I have been very interested in reading Aldous
Huxley's book *The Art of Seeing* that details the work of Dr.
William Bates on improving vision with eye relaxation
techniques.[8] The ideas are always helpful. I also noticed that
when Jesse began reading at 6 1/2 he often showed signs of
eyestrain -- rubbing his eyes, putting a hand over one eye, staring
hard and not blinking often enough. An eye check showed
nothing "wrong," but I still was very concerned. I began sharing

the Huxley ideas with Jesse. We both began palming our eyes before reading and in between each page. We tried to consciously blink much more frequently, and generally tried to relax and not stare and strain. It worked wonders. His reading began to come much more easily, he stopped showing stress, and began to be able to read for much longer times without any problems. This just might be another avenue for parents to look into when their children seem to have some eye and vision problem.

One of the basic ideas of Bates was that when we strain to see -- when we fear perhaps that the words might just fly off the page unless we nail them on with our eyeball -- *that's* when we see much worse. I think perhaps that many early readers might have that fear about the few tenuous words they feel they can read, a feeling similar to what John Holt described in *Never Too Late* when he went functionally blind when under the stress of reading music too fast:

> Suddenly something popped loose in my mind, and the written music before me lost all meaning. All meaning. It is hard to describe the experience, which lasted only a second or two. Strictly speaking, I could *see* the notes, I did not black out; but it was as if I could not see them. They were so blurred, as if my eyes were refusing to focus.[9]

I also remember seeing a photo somewhere of a classroom full of young Japanese children doing eye relaxation exercises before beginning their work for the day, so these ideas are being used in other parts of the world...

## Learning the Alphabet

**The first stage of learning to read ends when the child can recognize a letter quickly without having to think about which letter it is. At the same time that children are learning the alphabet they often learn to read about fifty or sixty sight words -- of course usually starting with his own name, a word of special meaning! When he knows the alphabet, he can read words just as easily if they are written in lower case or in capital letters.**

Incidentally, it is not necessary for children to know the names of the letters in order for them to know the alphabet. Some of the best phonics programs teach the letters by teaching their sounds rather than their names.

There are many ways that children learn the alphabet at home. Perhaps the most common is through an alphabet book. Since most homeschooling parents read to their children beginning shortly after the children are born, it is a natural step to read alphabet books. When the children are learning the letters they often want to hear such books over and over again.

Although many alphabet books are quite boring, some are quite humorous. My favorite is *Curious George Learns the Alphabet* by H. A. Rey. When Molly and Jacob were learning the alphabet, they loved to hear about the mischievous monkey, *Curious George*, being taught the alphabet by the *man with the yellow hat*. Not only does the book teach both capital and small letters by incorporating them into pictures, but it also maintains a fun spirit. As soon as George learns the letters up to *T*, he crosses out the word "one" on a message he takes to the baker and replaces it with the word "ten." Then he returns home with ten dozen doughnuts. The kids never fail to laugh when the *man with the yellow hat* says, "Well, that comes from teaching the alphabet to a little monkey. And I told you: no tricks!"

Many home-schoolers keep magnetized metal alphabet letters on their refrigerators. Children become more familiar with letter shapes when they manipulate them. Sometimes, when our children are in the beginning stages of reading, we spell out short messages on the refrigerator with these letters, or encourage them to sort them out or put them in alphabetical order. They are also useful to graphically show how some letters can be "flipped" to make another letter -- *u* becomes *n*, *b* becomes *q*. And some can be turned any way and still come out right, such as *o*.

I recommend that every family with beginning readers in

the house get or make an alphabet and put it up on a convenient wall in the house so that their beginning readers can frequently look at old letters that they already know when they are learning new letters. That way they can more easily learn to tell the letters apart from each other. These don't have to be the standard green chalkboard letters seen in drab elementary classrooms -- our kids have enjoyed whimsical alphabets that have the letters made out of objects or animals that begin with that letter's sound, or woodcut illustrations of farm themes for each letter. Some families put up the *Sing, Spell, Read & Write* alphabet that goes with the program's first phonics song. Cutting out letters together from magazines or newspapers, large easy to see letters, could be a fun joint project. Susan once found a set of thrown away billboard posters and made a wild alphabet using these huge, brightly colored letters. Madalene Murphy says her kids all learned the alphabet first from a needlepoint tapestry she'd made of all the letters and hung in their rooms.

When Jesse was just five, Susan wrote about an idea that worked for helping Jesse learn the alphabet...

I'm very interested in staying clear of workbook-type prepared "reading readiness" materials, feeling that the real world holds much more that is valuable and inherently motivating and intriguing. This is an idea that cost us nothing but scotch tape (Oh how *many* rolls of scotch tape!) and has brought us much delight and good sharing.

Things really began last winter. One day I began stapling together a 26-page booklet (my printer's scraps again), marking one alphabet letter on each page. Jesse, just 4 1/2, and his 6 year old friend asked what I was doing (cardinal rule #1 with me -- never come on as the "heavy" who has a super idea for a neat "*lesson*"). I explained that I planned to search through old magazines to find as many different types of alphabet letters as I could, taping each on to their proper pages in my book. I set to work nearby and they watched as they wanted. Jesse's friend wanted to make a book too, and soon even Jesse decided perhaps it might be fun. The idea didn't exactly "catch fire," though, so I let it be.

It was maybe TWO MONTHS later that this planted seed began to bear fruit and four months later we're still going strong. Out of the blue, Jesse asked to make a *new* alphabet book. He hadn't forgotten the idea, even though I'd thought it was a "dud" of sorts at the time. We counted pages, marked in letters, gathered magazines, and tape, and immediately were engrossed for over an hour. (What is it people say about young children's short attention spans???) Fat *A*'s, curling *G*'s, innumerable *E*'s, and snaking *S*'s began filling our new pages. Our eyes were opening to the vast creativity of the modern type-case. What variety! Jesse began noticing on his own that some letters were *very* hard to find, including his natural favorite, *J*. He began to cut off, secretly, the bottom foot from some capital *E*'s, as we were having such a hard time finding any *F*'s.

The letters began taking on personalities for us -- we talked of "that old *E*" that always was sneaking into so many words, half the time not even making any sound at all. We laughed about *T* always wearing his hat, but *J* changing his mind all the time about his. *A* and *H* always wore belts, but not *V*. We noticed the variations in lower-case printed *g* and *a*, and discussed the differences between handwritten letters and machine printed letters. We simply *had* to make motoring "RRRUM" sounds when we turned to our *R* page -- how different it was from our hissing, quiet *S* page. And we counted letters, compared pages to estimate which held the most, and Jesse wasn't fooled by letters that just took up more *space*. He realized he'd have to count to see which *really* had more. We saw how stocky and wide *M* was -- took up much more than twice the space as skinny *I*.

Jesse even now has begun to notice he can *read* some of the words he's finding in these magazines -- "Look: This says *NO*!" After finding and cutting out a few more words he knew, he said, "Gee! I didn't know they'd have *these* words in here!" It was a banner day when *Time* magazine ran a cover story on *Jesse Helms...*

Jesse has gone back to this idea throughout the summer. One morning while Jacob slept in unusually late, we must have worked a solid 2 hours at it, and went back to it later that afternoon -- all at Jesse's request. We work as partners at it, taking turns cutting or taping in. It's not an assignment I've given him to complete, but a shared adventure *in* the real world of print. I've become as excited as my 5- year-old to find a really unique letter (our favorites are the Meow- Mix cat food letters), or that rare treasure of treasures, a real *Q*. (We joked that probably there were no *Q*'s because there weren't very many advertisements for *quick, quiet, quaint Queens...*)

I've secretly bought Jesse a copy of *Modern Display Alphabets*, by Paul Kennedy, from John Holt's book list, and wonder if I'll be able to keep it hidden until Christmas. Jesse is trying his hand at making some "fancy" letters himself -- some with bulby serifs, or rainbow stripes, some very tall or very short. He's even begun a game of pretending he's a printer, and he'll make signs to order for anyone in the house. We notice the world of print all about us, and laugh about wanting to cut out letters from signs we pass while out driving.

And, ah, how different this adventure of ours has been from the dutiful, dreadfully dull filling in of kindergarten workbook pages... And little Jacob sits next to us blissfully taping letters into *his* alphabet book, chanting to himself about how the Mommy *A* will nurse the Baby *a...*

### Learning The First Words

**Children can learn letters as they learn words. They can easily learn to recognize fifty or sixty words even before they are fully familiar with the alphabet. In *Teacher*, one of the most enthusiastic books ever written about the teaching of reading, Sylvia Ashton-Warner allows each of her students to choose a special word to learn each day. The children, many of them Maori Indian children of New Zealand, would think of a word that meant a lot to them -- "Mommy,"**

"love," "skeleton," and so on -- and their teacher would put the word on a card for their special collection. When Jesse was about five and a half years old, Susan began to put words that he would choose on little cards. They invented several cooperative go-fish type games with them, or simple sentence making games, Jesse gaining more familiarity and ease with the words as they played.

When I used to teach remedial reading to second grade students, I would ask each child to choose words which I then put on 3 by 5 index cards using a crayon or magic marker -- a different color marker for each child in the class. Once a week, we would play a game which we called "Sorry." I would shuffle all of the students' words together and add in some cards on which the word *sorry* was written. Then we would take turns choosing cards and saying the words written on them. If we would pick the word "sorry," we would have to pass all our cards to the next person. It was a fun way to learn words.

### Nicole Learns to Read Using Wordcards

One home-schooling mother, Juanita Kissell, told me about how her daughter Nicole started reading using wordcards when she was five and a half and just about to enter kindergarten.

One day, Juanita saw Nicole staring at the words in a book called *Snow* that they had gotten out of the library several times. Juanita pointed and said, "Do you know what that word is?"

"Snow?" guessed Nicole.

"Yes," Juanita replied. "Do you know that when you know what the word says, THAT'S reading."

"Oh? Oh!" Nicole was surprised. She thought that reading was more complicated than that.

"Is there any word you'd like to read?"

"Yeah!"

So Nicole started choosing words and Juanita started writing them down on cards. Pretty soon, Nicole had a collection of about thirty words, mainly nouns, on cards. She liked to get them out every day.

One day Juanita said, "You know, if we add a couple of more words we could make a sentence out of them." That day the words, *in* and *the*, were added and Juanita and Nicole laid out the cards and made a few sentences.

Within three or four weeks Nicole had about 150 words on cards. Then they started making silly sentences like "The cat is purple." Juanita would make a sentence and Nicole would read it, then Nicole would make a sentence and Juanita would read it. The chance to make funny, nonsensical sentences from these simple words, to create humor out of mere words on cards, would have Nicole laughing out loud -- and loving her beginning reading times at home.

One day after Nicole had about two hundred words, Juanita asked, "Would you like to try to read a book?" Nicole was excited, so, that day they got some Dr. Seuss books out of the library; Nicole read the words that she knew and her mother read the other words.

Nicole was attending a half-day kindergarten, so Juanita wondered if Nicole could begin to receive some reading instruction in school. She called the school to find out what was available, as she could see how eager Nicole was and how readily she was catching on. The very next day, without warning, the school decided to give Nicole a reading readiness test. Nicole got very uncomfortable when a strange man pulled her out of class to give her this unexpected test, and she failed it.

Juanita began homeschooling Nicole in first grade. When I saw Nicole in March of that year, she was reading books like *Ramona the Pest* by Beverly Cleary, which are miles beyond the usual first grade fare.

**Simple Games for Learning Words**

**Susan made up lots of simple games which helped Jesse learn his first words, as she described when Jesse was five...**

As Jesse has always found great delight in spinning off reels of rhyming words, we began making simple rhyming flip books. You'll need some small blank cards -- index card size, printer's scraps, whatever. Cut most of the cards in half, and staple these on top of one full size card, as shown:

As you flip through the book, a different rhyming word pops up -- seems almost magical to a beginning reader that one letter makes the change. Jesse helps in thinking up words for these books -- especially enjoys inventing silly-sounding nonsense words. Jacob (2 1/2) has even had good fun with the idea -- not in reading the words, of course, but in thinking up his own rhyming combinations. He thinks it's a great joke to ask for "cinnamon-jinnamon-binnamon" for his breakfast oatmeal, loving to twirl the funny words on his tongue, laughing. Jesse notices rhymes everywhere, often saying, "Hey, that would make a good flip book!"

Another game that's evolved is the "Message Game," played with our refrigerator magnetic letters. Jesse is now in charge of alphabetizing the letters every Monday, and scrounging up lost ones from under the refrigerator. This usually takes him about the same time as my breakfast cleanup, and so gives us both some work to do in the kitchen, (Always good to have company during jobs!) First the message is arranged -- our usual favorite starting one that Jesse *always* can read is "Give Mommy a HUG." Then the message is changed to perhaps "Give Mommy a RUG" or "BUG" or "JUG." Jesse must run to get me these things from about the house. Soon, it's Jesse's turn to write *me* a message. (I'm never allowed to look while he's writing *his*, so I can often do another bit of needed neatening during this time...) He usually likes to use his favorite books to help him with spelling out words he needs, coming up with "Give Jesse a dinosaur," etc., and then I must find those items for *him*. He's reluctant to just try putting words together as they sound to him, but he does know that he has resources to turn to other than just me. The game goes on until Jesse wants to stop, often a half-hour or more (or other times 5 minutes!). It is full of lots of laughs, hugs, and sitting on laps and leaping about -- no quiet desk work for us!

Another idea that has been a help to us is making Jesse his own small word book-dictionary. We stapled together 26 long skinny pages, and wrote one letter at the top of each page. Anytime Jesse needs to spell a word, for a letter to Grandma, the message game, a sign he's making, a note to Daddy, etc., I'll write it in his book on the proper page. It's surprising how much learning comes from this simple device. First, of course, it saves all the innumerable scraps of paper we used to have lying about when Jesse wanted words written out for him -- helps cut down on clutter! Jesse always wants me to read over all his "old" words on a page whenever a new one is added, absorbing again the initial sounds of the words. Often a word he needs is already in his book and Jesse can usually somehow figure out which one it is. He's getting more familiar with alphabetical order, and is now able to find the letter for the word he needs without looking through the entire book randomly. He can also guess what letter his word will start with, and is always pleased when he comes up with a word for a letter page that hasn't had any words written on it up to then...

A Short History of Reading Instruction

One of the first reading methods used in this country, beginning in colonial times, was the "alphabet-spelling system" in which spelling instruction and reading instruction were the same thing. Children would learn to read by spelling out loud. Longer words would be spelled by syllables. For example, the word "attention" would be recited, "*A T, at, T E N, ten, T I O N, tion.*"

In *On the Banks of Plum Creek*, Laura learned to read by spelling. She was called up to the teacher's desk and began to learn to read by spelling and saying the words on the first line of her speller, *cat, pat, rat and mat.*[10]

In the 1830s, the *McGuffey Eclectic Readers* were first published, and pupils began to learn phonics.

Then, in the 1920's the "look-say" method became the predominant method. The idea was that children could learn to read without all of the difficulty involved with learning phonics. Soon, the Scott Foresman readers with Dick, Jane, and Sally swept the country.

Then, in 1955, Rudolf Flesch wrote *Why Johnny Can't Read* which held that many American children were failing to learn to read because they were not learning phonics. Flesch made quite a stir -- his book climbed to the top of the best-seller lists and stayed there. Up to that time, the American public had left reading instruction to the reading educators. Now the educators were on the defensive. Committees were formed. Research was conducted. New beginning- reading methods were tried...

Soon the time came to summarize the new research, to decide whether "phonics" or "look-say" was the better approach. In 1967, Jeanne Chall, mentioning Rudolf Flesch only briefly, concluded, as he had, that phonics (which she called "code-emphasis") was indeed more effective.[11]

### Fun With Dick and Jane

Chall's report was accepted by the majority of educators, and soon, the "look-say" readers were gathering dust. We happened upon a whole collection of those readers almost by accident. When Jacob was four and Molly fourteen months, a retired teacher friend of ours cleaned out her basement and gave us her old readers. Included were all of the editions of the king of the "look say" readers -- *Fun With Dick and Jane*. Two years later Susan wrote...

It's been a golden time for my middle child Jacob lately. Not only is he now SIX (and "as clever as clever"), but his two front teeth are out now, he's getting very proud of his soprano recorder ability, AND he's now really learning to read. And reading a BOOK, not just a spot of words here and there.

Now, I'm a trifle embarrassed to admit to some readers exactly what books it IS that have been Jacob's chosen entry into this new realm of the literary. You'll laugh, or you'll be aghast, or you'll be at least quite stunned, knowing my general disdain for most school textbooks, and school readers in particular. But here it is -- Jacob has begun reading, and become VERY excited about reading, by choosing as his own *We Look and See*, a 1947 version of the old Dick-Jane-Sally-Spot-Tim-Puff books... The real "look-say" pre-primer stuff I've always referred to as dumb, awful, disrespectful, horribly boring, the no-wonder-kids-hate-reading-in-school stuff. Jacob now loves them, they are HIS books. This piece is my wondering why, my sorting out, my sharing with you.

I've had a pet theory (formed when Jesse first became a reader a few years ago around age 6 1/2) that kids only like -- and enjoy and find amusing and worth endless re-readings -- all the very simple "first books" WHEN they view themselves as people actively learning to read. If instead they view themselves as LISTENERS foremost, then the easy books mean nothing, they are spurned and ignored in favor of the REALLY good stuff -- *Peter Pan*, *Heidi*, *Charlotte's Web*, The *Little House* books. Real literature, stories to immerse yourself in, and become and delight in. I saw this with Jesse -- all the I CAN READ BOOKS we had were crisp and new, unloved and un-dogged eared UNTIL Jesse became a beginning reader. Then they were all gathered into a special shelf in his bedroom, read, re-read, talked over, laughed over, seriously discussed, viewed from 20 different angles and insights. Thoroughly known and loved. Books just a cut above his current ability were referred to with a "Why, Jesse, I bet in just another two months you'll even be reading THIS!" It was a new adventure, a new falling in love.

And so I wondered what would do it for Jacob. What book would he claim as his personal ticket? Looking back, his choice seems entirely understandable, even predictable (if still amusing and charming in its innocence...). You see, these old Dick-Jane-and-Sally books are really family treasures now. We've ALL fallen in love with them.

We first got these books two years ago. I recognized them right off as being very close to the versions I'd read as a 6 year old (and links with our own past always carry wide emotional ties, stronger than we know maybe). We all looked through them, laughing at how DUMB the stories were, how clipped and short the language, how ALL hard (and interesting) words were carefully deleted and how almost any situation could be responded to with "Oh, oh, oh! Funny, funny _____!" But besides laughing over the books we also realized they could come in handy. After all, they had BABY SALLY in them, and Molly, then not quite one and a half, loved BABIES in her books. Maybe we could distract and absorb Molly with them, and so get on with our own more important work. And for Molly it was love at first sight -- unabashed, immediate, undying to this day (OUR love has grown much more slowly, to be sure!). Molly hugged (and lugged) these books about, chanting "Baby! Baby!" with a far off look of wonderment in her eyes. Utterly smitten. And we had to admit that Baby Sally did remind US a good bit of Molly -- same chubby good spirits, same absorption in things like carefully daubing bath powder all over herself and all her toys and pets, or trying to stuff kittens into baby swings... And Jesse, just then turned 7, and just beginning to become a SOMEWHAT comfortable and fluent reader, would sometimes offer to read Molly ALL of the three Dick-Jane pre-primers, plus all of the longer first book straight through, and I'd be amused to see him chuckling aloud over the books, really enjoying the EASE of this reading and the humor in these ridiculous non-stories.

And we even did a good bit of "Critical Comparison" with the readers that were used in those days. We compared "Dick and Jane" to "Dot and Jim," and "Janet and John," and "Susan and Ted" -- all the other similar 3 children in a nondescript happy family basal readers. We came to the conclusion that, of books of this particular genre (not that we LIKED the genre, mind you!) the "Dick and Janes" were indeed the best. We compared the more recent mid 1950's versions to the 1947, to the 1939, to the 1926. We had them all, and laughed over the changes we saw over the years. Also definitely noticed the lowering of word count -- the same "plot" would become more and more truncated over time, eventually winding up with no nouns at all, and very top heavy with "oh, oh, oh!"

Now Jacob always most vociferously has labelled these books as stupid and dumb, has flown into innumerable rages when Molly has insisted we read her one of these when HE wanted a REAL story book read. That's of course all changed now. Jesse "mentioned" this to Jacob at supper tonight, saying, "But Jacob, I thought you always used to HATE these books." (He received a swift kick under the table from me and a scathing glance and he quickly changed the subject...) Jacob's response was utter disbelief and shock -- hate HIS BOOKS? NEVER!!

I can't even now actually remember how it was that Jacob suddenly took to these books. It WAS sudden, it was on one particular day. The timing was somehow right, if unplanned. It was as if Jacob suddenly looked at this print and could suddenly apprehend and grasp the whole idea of reading, a real "aha!" experience for him. The sort that made him grab the book from me and point to the words eagerly HIMSELF, able now to

READ, even if it was just "oh, oh, oh." From that day on, we've been always referring to Jacob as "someone who's REALLY learning to read," and we tell everyone else this and he overhears, and he's readily viewing himself in this way, too. Not that he thinks he's completed the process, or become fluent, or become cocky about the whole thing -- it's just that he's readily identifying himself as someone capably going down this long road, he's begun the journey, and feels momentum and a good swing to his step. HE'S moving down the road, he's not being dragged, he's not lost, and not taking too many bad falls. (One somewhat "bad fall" was the day recently when he announced he WOULDN'T read his DICK AND JANE that day, instead he'd read an Arnold Lobel FROG AND TOAD book. He quickly saw he was way over his head, and the discouragement was palpable.)

Now our actual way of using these books is far different from the typical school scenario of the Round Robin reading circle. Jacob knows he'll read to me daily (and I try to be very consistent in not letting a day slip by -- only takes 5 to 10 minutes, after all). He sits on my lap in an old stuffed rocker, cuddled back against me, and he begins. Usually he starts at the beginning of the book each time. "Oh, oh, oh!" and on and on. He points a finger at each word, usually, barely glancing at the picture. He's clearly not just reciting, as he used to do last winter when he "read" *Harry the Kitten* by spouting whole long passages without a glance at the text -- or maybe a finger running under each line in proper left to right sequence but with his eyes completely feasting on the pictures. He makes mistakes, he mis-reads, AND HE CORRECTS HIMSELF -- all without the terrible abuse of fellow reading group mates ready to pounce on any error with urgently upraised hands. And he even uses his growing phonics knowledge with these books. We did lots of informal phonics work last winter -- matching beginning sounds of words, beginning to write by Jacob sounding words out as best he could, making rhyming flip books, talking and laughing about "roaring Richman R" and "leg of lamb L" and "SSSSnaky

S." He became much more tuned into thinking of sounds in words, more noticing, and so he brings all this to these unabashedly sight word oriented books. We continue to do more phonics work, as play, on the side, but for Jacob THIS is real reading -- the work of reading a text with a STORY.

We usually try to read in the morning when Jacob is freshest, and when Jesse is off quiet in the livingroom reading on his own. Molly usually wants to crawl up and listen, too, (remember these were first "her" books) and this is sometimes tolerated by Jacob, sometimes not. Molly never tires of hearing these books, and is even claiming now that SHE can read them, too. Jacob feels very superior and grown-up because he KNOWS he's doing the real thing and that Molly is just pretending. (Actually I don't think it will be all that long until Molly is NOT just pretending, but that's another story...)

And too, for Jacob it is very comforting and necessary and good that the books are so easy. Lots of repetition, and no tongue-twisting mix-ups like the ones found in some strict linguistic or phonics readers. You know, the "Can Dan fan Nan? Pat can fan Dan. Can Nan fan a fat man?" sort of thing. I think Jacob's tongue would get in hopeless knots quickly and he'd burst into tears over such stuff.

A friend recently said to me she couldn't understand why all the "first" readers all repeated things so much. Why not ONE "jump," instead of "jump, jump, jump?" Well, for Jacob it was quite an enlightening thing to realize that if he'd read a word once, and the same constellation of letters came up again, right away, that it WAS THE SAME WORD. He'd be able to tell it at a glance -- the SAME WORD! -- and so get a feeling of speed to his reading, right away.

Jacob is also free to make fun of these books when he feels like it. Today he came up to me laughing, with his arms outstretched and all his fingers spread wide apart. He told me he was acting as if HE were one of the Dick-Jane illustrations -- they are almost always drawn in various states of shock, FINGERS OUTSPREAD (the physical counterpart of "oh, oh, oh" I guess...). A few times, especially if the days reading is hard, or Jacob is feeling a bit grumpy about the whole thing, Jacob will suddenly decide to read every person's name or pet's name as "dumb." "Go, Dumb, go! Run, Dumb, run!" Funny thing is, of course, he has to read all the names silently to himself FIRST to even figure out they are names -- it's actually quite a mental trick for him, and a game he enjoys immensely. We don't have to pretend we always feel enraptured with Dick and Jane's exploits -- although amazingly enough we actually do enjoy them a bit and are often surprised to find ourselves laughing aloud over them.

These books also give Jacob a clear direction -- they're not a dead-end, one story proposition. He's seriously set himself the goal of reading through the whole of the first Primer (it follows the three preprimers he's working on now) by Christmas -- or sooner. We refer to his books as "chapter books" (albeit very short chapters, of course...) and talk about the whole SERIES, and Jacob views his work with them with the same seriousness of purpose as Jesse's goal of reading all the *Little House* books on HIS own. They now each have their own series, their own turf of equal dimension.

And Jacob, whose forte is NOT sociability and outward friendliness, let alone TALKATIVENESS with others, has come out of his awkwardness a bit through his new reading ability. One night, at 9:30 p.m. when I was feeling overwhelmed that I hadn't YET begun getting everyone up to bed but was letting us slip into another late night/late morning cycle -- just then Jacob announced sturdily that he wanted to go and read to "Pap Pap," his grandfather. Now Jacob has rarely said out right that he wanted to do ANYTHING with ANYONE, and so when Jacob said this, we all acted. We got Molly back into her clothes, got shoes on everyone, and walked up to the cottage, and Jacob read to his grandmother and grandfather, cuddled on his Pap Pap's lap. They were charmed and amazed -- perhaps partly amazed because they'd never heard him utter so many words so clearly in all his life. This good event also spurred Jesse on to prepare his OWN book to read to his grandparents, something he never would have thought of doing on his own -- a good example of a younger sibling inspiring an older, rather than always the other way around.

We've also begun forming little rituals to mark special reading accomplishments. Jacob requested I make him a small stuffed toy cat when he completed the first preprimer, and I agreed, and even followed through on it. I'm often a great PROMISER of homemade toys, but often just don't quite get to the sewing machine to really make the plans realities... So this follow-through on BOTH our parts -- Jacob in reading, me in sewing -- was very good for us and our relationship. Bribery? I don't think so. I see it more as just a concrete way to help Jacob recognize and feel proud of his own accomplishments. A sort of "graph" of his progress.

And Jacob now has his first official books listed on his "Stairway of Books," opposite Jesse's. He's moving along, and I'm sure he'll soon become as voracious a reader as his brother.

Now, I hope no one interprets this piece as a "recommendation" of "DICK AND JANE." They would probably bomb out completely in most families and with most kids. I hope more just to encourage all of you to be ready to respond to YOUR child's way of moving into reading, and be ready to appreciate the work they do, the problems they need to overcome, and respect the materials THEY choose from what you make available. And I hope you can take the time to DELIGHT in your child's beginning reading accomplishments and triumphs, get beyond all the doubts about "proper" methods and just really see and appreciate our own unique kids. HAPPY READING!

# 4. Learning Phonics

The longest, hardest, task for children, when they are learning to read, is learning phonics -- the relationships between written words and spoken words.

Often, when children are beginning to connect letters and sounds, they will notice sounds in the words that they see. For example, recently Jacob said, "Did you know that the *PH* in *Murphys* makes the *F* sound?" Usually, the links that Jacob notices are accurate, sometimes they are not.

When Jacob was just beginning to make these connections, Susan wrote...

Jacob is making beginning steps towards reading and it's very exciting. I'm watching him begin forging new links, new hypotheses, tumbling ideas about in his 5 year old mind till he's brave enough and sure enough to show me his little polished gems of discovery. Today, en route to the Western Pennsylvania La Leche League Conference, in the midst of other conversations that he wasn't part of, he suddenly piped up with, "Mommy! the word *juice* starts with *B*!!!" He was obviously very proud, very confident, repeated his discovery a few times. Now usually when Jacob makes these observations he's right, or close (like, "Mommy, *elephant* begins with *L*"). But today it was "*juice* begins with *B*." How was I to respond? Several choices sprang before me, rather like an array of possible answers on a multiple choice test. I could:

1. Rain on his parade -- say, perhaps sadly, obviously pained at his ignorance, that, no, *juice* didn't start with *B*, sweety, it started with *J*, can't you hear it?

2. I could laugh and ridicule his conclusion (as I

feared Jesse might -- luckily he wasn't listening at all as he was utterly absorbed in reading the final blizzard scene in *On the Banks of Plum Creek*).

3. I could give Jacob an impromptu and frantic phonics drill on *J* vs. *B* sounds, worried that he might be showing signs of something worse than even dyslexia -- he not only confuses *D* and *B*, but *J* and *B*!

4. Or I could respond as I did, saying, "Wow, Jacob, you are really thinking about the sounds you hear in lots of words, all on your own!"

5. Or I could have responded with none of the above, ignoring his proud comment as not worth noticing or "reinforcing," and just get back to my discussion with Howard.

I could have tossed aside Jacob's little brave gem as mere muddy gravel. I think that must happen a lot when we respond carelessly to our children, or too anxiously or too seriously. I'm glad that today I didn't do that to Jacob. There will be time enough for him to rethink, rework, reconsider, time enough to point out the *J* on the orange juice can the next time he mixes up a batch...

### Dealing With Children's Frustrations

Perhaps the key to how quickly children will learn phonics is how much time they are willing to put into trying to sound out words. If they are willing to spend five or ten seconds of effort each time they come to a new word, they will probably make quick progress. If they are only willing to spend about one second and then they start searching the ceiling for the answer, then they won't learn very quickly.

Many children get very tense when they are trying to sound-out words. If they get frustrated, and don't think that they can succeed no matter how hard they try, they will spend less and less time trying.

If you listen to a beginning reader, sometimes you can

hear the tension. I was talking to a mother of a late reader this weekend. I had tested Laura when she was seven and just getting started. Now, three years later, I gave her another test and she was reading at an average level for a ten-year-old. She also was starting to read long chapter books to herself. It was clear that she was well on her way to becoming an excellent reader. Laura's mother said that Laura's reading voice had recently changed. It used to sound stilted and tense. Her baby brother, imitating her, would pretend to read in the same voice. But now, it was smooth and relaxed.

My kids frequently experience frustrations with learning, especially my boys, Jesse (now 10) and Jacob (now 7). Molly (just turning four) meets challenges usually with more ease and equanimity, but she too has her times of personal outrage and trauma when things don't come easily. Mostly for Molly, however, things just DO seem to come more easily -- her coordination is more mature and ready, she can remember more effortlessly, she is eager. And because she is young, she is not pushed or coerced into trying things that might be beyond her.

One thing I have definitely noticed about both boys -- they seem to thrive on some structure to their days, some "inner skeleton" to our daily lives and our joint expectations. If I just let things slide and don't ask them to take part in certain things regularly with me, then I meet all sorts of frustrations and anger and groans and arguments when I eventually suggest the activity again.

Take recorder playing with Jacob. When we play regularly, we develop a rhythm, a "game" as it were, of how we should go about the music time. Jacob gets better and better (VERY gradually, mind you), less frustrated with himself, and I find my own creativity flowing in finding new ways to help us go about it all. BUT when we slide, and let days, and even weeks, go by without our special music time together, then it is like going back to square one, or perhaps minus three. Jacob can clearly and painfully realize that he no longer is as good as he was just a short while back, his fingers are clumsy, he slouches and groans, furrows his forehead, audibly moans and complains. It is always VERY tempting when this happens to just lay off entirely, just forget the whole idea of playing music with Jacob, just say to myself that he is not "ready" and to try again in a year (or three, or never). But somehow the memory of the good times we've had won't let me do that, and so I persevere. I try again the next day, and often it is more of the same. But we try the next day, and somehow then it's NOT so bad. Maybe I'm working harder at being more patient, more focused on Jacob's successes, more trying to remember the ATMOSPHERE of our good times and how we achieved that. Things start once again moving along somewhat positively. Less groaning, less complaining, more enthusiasm. Soon Jacob is taking more control of the situation, deciding how we'll structure the day's time -- "First I'll play five *Cats in the Cradles*, then five *Hot Cross Buns*, then five *Mary Had a Little Lambs*, then..." We both begin having a good time of it, and look forward to playing recorder together as an expectation in our day. We get back in our rhythm, and can move forward.

I remember Donald Graves saying in *Write From the Start*, a wonderful book on writing with children, that if children write only one day a week, then they will always balk at that one time. But if children begin to write regularly, almost daily, THEN they can begin to feel like real writers, feel some momentum, some rhythm to it all. They can begin to feel a part of a long process, less worried about each day's little troubles and frustrations. With very irregular writing, they are so focused on that one effort, which may be turning out VERY poorly, and they can't see beyond that. ALL writers turn out LOTS of stuff that they look back on and decide to toss -- but if you have LOTS of writing, many days and MONTHS of writing, you also find some gems worth polishing in the pile. You can start to realize that each day's particular effort is not so earth shattering, that it's the cumulative body of work that becomes important.

I've seen this so clearly with Jesse. Jesse has written a lot over these several years, but he too has times when he's "off" writing. Summer usually does it (like now...), because there just isn't time to do such a sit-down type of activity when there are the woods inviting play, and treehouse building, or haymaking to help with, or the pond to swim in. Summer is a different time, and I usually respect that writing just can't take place much then. But soon fall will be here, and we'll start in again. I expect he'll feel rusty, creaky in the joints from disuse. He'll probably have trouble zeroing in on a topic, probably have trouble writing thoughts with any fluency or speed, probably leave out all punctuation and capital letters and seem to have regressed terribly in spelling. He'll probably groan about it all, I'll probably be demanding and critical and impatient, but I feel certain we'll make it. I feel confident we'll get over that initial hurdle. We'll probably spend some time rereading lots of his old writing from last year and the year before, just to get a feel for where he was when he "left off." We'll make a new writing folder, decide on what types of paper or notebooks he wants to write rough drafts in, or if he's going to focus on typing with our word-processor. We'll probably try to set goals together for writing ideas, brainstorming together about topics, styles of writing he might want to try, new places to submit finished pieces. I'm sure the good rhythm of daily writing won't be especially easy to work into, but we'll keep at it. It's what we expect to do now come Fall. I'm trusting our memories of the good writing done in the past will spur us on, get us over those first bad days.

I think that one thing dealing with my kids' frustrations has taught me is that we can't give up. We can't say, "Oh, they just WON'T do it, I give up on them." We become what John Holt always described as "serious" teachers -- we look for other ways to go about it all, try to observe the situation more clearly, read what others have done to get a fresh perspective, step back a bit to get our bearings and then try again. We make changes, we negotiate. We accept the frustration and then move on from there. We try again. We try NOT to just blame the KIDS for all the trouble.

I've also found, in working with our kids, that it always helps for ME to be actively working at learning something new also, so that I can share with the kids my own difficulties and frustrations and how I'm going at working them out. Helps with piano with Jesse. For a month or more I hadn't really tried seriously learning a new piece -- instead I had been working at polishing up some oldies. But I was asking HIM to consider a new piece, quite a hard one for him, "Short Story" in the *Suzuki* Book Two. And sometimes I would push him beyond his endurance or capabilities, wanting to work on everything in the piece at once, wanting him to keep at it for far longer than he could bear. It's helped tremendously now for me to be working on a new piece (the last "Minuet" by Bach in the *Suzuki* Book Two), and to realize again how HARD it is to get a new piece together. I know again the frustration of getting ONE hand going the right way, but it all falls apart when I add the OTHER hand. It takes slowing down, breaking the piece down into smaller bits, ignoring the second half of the piece just now till I get the first part more in control. Getting a feel of the piece humming through my head. Now I'm more empathetic and responsive with Jesse and his limits and needs, because I'm feeling all of this in myself again. My better approach is not just an abstraction, not something I read in a book about a "positive" way to deal with children -- I'm responding now out of my own experience.

Same goes for writing -- when I write, then I can better help Jesse and Jacob write. When I'm out of touch with my own writing, then I'm not much good at getting in touch with their work either. Instead I'm impatient, badgering, looking over their shoulders with a frown, ready to pounce. Expecting instant perfection. (Often when I'M "off" writing is exactly when the boys are "off" writing, so we're ALL out of rhythm, out of sync...) When I am involved in my own work, then I can share with the boys more as a COLLEAGUE, not come on just as a dictator of sorts, or a nasty judge. I can listen better, feel into their way of working more.  Maybe I feel more humbled when I'm writing too, or more excited, or just more active myself.

Another thing that has helped us a lot is to notice the weather and what it's doing when we're all feeling particularly close to tears all day and frustrations break out into nasty accusations too frequently.  Most specifically we try to notice the air pressure.  Last winter we did a stint of reading about weather and made several weather detecting devices.  I began reading in a *TIME/LIFE* book about the many experiments that have been done to see what affect changes in air pressure have on animals and people, and it was fascinating.  Seems low air pressure makes even pets fussy and fidgety and snappish, and with people -- watch out!  Studies have shown that students in schools are much more unruly and have more trouble concentrating during low air pressure times.  Tempers snap, everything seems too hard, too overwhelming, too frustrating.  Give a change to high pressure, and everything seems more even, more manageable, more possible, and everyone concentrates better.  Now around here even Molly can be heard to say, "Watch out, it must be a low air pressure day!" if she can tell everyone is getting on everyone's nerves too much.  I'm thinking of buying a good barometer this fall, so we can all keep track of air pressure changes ourselves more accurately, and so become more understanding of our mood changes, less blaming each other personally for bad days.  Maybe realize that the bad days are indeed bad DAYS, not an indication of bad PEOPLE.

Another thing that I think will help long-term in helping the kids through frustrating learning times is that we read a LOT of biographies, short and long, about inventors and scientists.  And the kids are clearly getting at least one very important message from them -- these folks DIDN'T give up easily, even in the face of seemingly endless frustration.  The invention of velcro took TEN YEARS (the inspiration was burrs caught on a dogs' fur...).  The zipper took even more.  And we all know about Edison's sleepless nights, night after night, when he was working at finding a proper filament for his lightbulb idea.  Galileo and

Newton kept at grinding lenses for telescopes for months on end, and sometimes had to then abandon the lens if it wasn't just right. The Wright brothers had many more than a dozen flops before successfully getting off the ground. And so it made me feel good the other day when Jacob came up and said, "What if the man who invented zippers had just given up after one year?" They are realizing that it IS possible to keep going even with long-term frustration, that an idea may take a very long time to come to fruition, that the great people of the world who have made positive changes weren't put off by initial roadblocks and dead-ends. The old "try, try again" saying really applied to these folks, and I think my kids will internalize this more and more over time. At least our reading is giving them a more realistic model for dealing with initial or continuing frustration than that found in most schools. In school it is usually, "Get it right, right now, or else." No second chances, let alone tenth or hundredth chances, no chance to keep at something hard for years on end. It's get it NOW, or we'll list you as "failed" forever.

In this connection, I was amused by an incident the other day when I was visiting homeschooler Carol Wilson in Pittsburgh. During an extra moment I tried playing my Clementi Sonatina on their piano (one of my "polishing up" pieces that still needs some polishing...). Carol's son Luke (almost 9) heard the music, and Carol overheard him say to Jesse, "Wow! What is she playing! That's not even ON my Suzuki tape! That sounds REALLY hard!" Now Carol has often said that Luke feels terribly frustrated with anything if he can't get it perfectly the very first time he tries it, and she thinks maybe Jesse was trying to help Luke feel less overwhelmed by my seeming "mastery" by replying, "Oh, yes, but she's been working on that piece for over a year now."

And it's true, I have been. And I'm sure I'll be working on it still next year, and Jesse knows this. Jesse overhears my practice times, hears me talking about my pieces, hears me stumble over particularly hard parts, knows how I backslide if I don't practice regularly, AND he hears me get better gradually over time. He knows I don't give it all up just because it's hard. He also knows it's not "magic" that I can do what I can now do; he knows I've worked at it a long while, for hours and hours and hours over several years. He knows maybe that people have to EARN their accomplishments. Good long-term thing to know...

## Using a Phonics Program

**Many homeschooled children learn phonics through a parent-directed program which teaches them how to sound out words. After Jacob had read several versions of the Dick and Jane pre-primers and had a reading vocabulary of perhaps one hundred words, we purchased** *Sing, Spell, Read & Write* **by Sue Dickson,[1] an attractive, though expensive, phonics program including cassette tapes, workbooks, games, and beginning readers. In a matter of months, six year old Jacob moved through the beginning readers and took off into reading other easy reading books and rereading his Dick and Jane primers with a new eye. As Susan writes...**

I first heard about this phonics/beginning reading program from a flyer in the mail a year and a half ago or so. Looked mildly interesting -- seemed to have cassette tapes of songs to help kids learn phonics generalizations, a bunch of games, a set of paper-back readers. Seemed to be specially suited to home use, too, although it had been developed for use first in a school setting. The $90.00 price tag put me off -- AND the notion that I NEEDED such a pre-set-up "program" to help my kids with beginning reading. Afterall, Jesse had become a competent reader without such nonsense. So I probably tossed the flyer out, although I was wondering if anyone else had ever used it or heard of it.

Then came our second legislative breakfast in Harrisburg to lobby for our Home Education Bill. The *Sing, Spell, Read & Write* folks were there for our "mini-conference" afterwards to

---

[1] Available from CBN Publishing, The Christian Broadcasting Network, Inc., Virginia Beach, VA 23465-9989, phone: 800-288-4769.

give a talk and demonstrate their materials. And so I met Sue Dickson, the woman who actually developed *SSRW*, a former elementary school teacher. She was delightful, really seemed to be a creative, vivacious person who genuinely was excited about finding ways to make beginning reading easier for kids. She said that she'd realized how hard it was for her students to remember phonics generalizations with the usual materials -- in one ear, out the other, all with a yawn.

She HAD noticed that kids seemed to be able to remember favorite SONGS easily -- jingles for commercials, jumprope chants, folksongs. Songs didn't seem like "work" for most kids -- they were easy, a breeze. So Sue began putting these ideas together, and came up with simple songs about letters and their sounds and combinations. Then she wrote little phonics readers to go with them, cumulatively adding on all the sounds a child had come across, added simple BINGO-type games and Go-Fish matching card games, some "raceway" charts for a child to keep track of their progress, and *Sing, Spell, Read & Write* was born.

I wasn't able to sit in on all of Sue Dickson's presentation, as I was leading another workshop discussion at the same time, but I caught the tail end, and had a chance to hear some of the phonics songs. My first reaction to the songs was that they were certainly not particularly great music -- in fact they were down right sing-songy and "canned." BUT my kids and I found ourselves humming and singing these few songs we'd heard for several MONTHS afterward -- they WERE catchy, and we'd been caught. Over the next few months I had a chance to see the *SSRW* materials several times when other homeschooling mothers were sharing them with friends (how useful it is to actually see educational materials, away from a salesperson, and also hear how some others are using them). I liked some of the game ideas, heard more of the tapes, even peeked in the readers and saw they weren't awful. But we still didn't buy the program ourselves.

Jacob, then age 6, began reading that fall using "Dick and Jane" readers. He certainly knew most consonant sounds and sounds of most short vowels from informal work we'd been doing for a good while -- most especially in writing with our computer -- but at some point it all got overwhelming. He was mostly using first letters and general look and shape and feel of a word to recognize words he'd met, with a heavy dose of context clues. He had a growing vocabulary, and was excited about reading, but his reading vocabulary was limited to only those words he'd already specifically come across in his stories.

Jacob couldn't generate new words from old ones -- he couldn't take *jump* and so figure out the new word *dump*, or take *look* and turn it into *book*. And he definitely couldn't sound out a simple short vowel word like *bag* -- he'd get all mixed up about the whole IDEA of sounding out a word, trying to fit in letter NAMES instead of sounds, and generally getting in a dither (and on particularly bad days, not just a dither but something bordering on a tantrum...). He wanted nothing to do with my improvised phonics games with known words, and he got utterly mixed up and angry when I tried to use some ideas from some other phonics books around the house. He was getting frustrated; I was getting frustrated. We needed a change, and I began wondering again about *SSRW*.

Our good homeschooling friends the Basemans purchased *SSRW* that winter, and shared a set of the phonics song tapes with us. At first I was surprised that there were only about 8 actual songs on the tapes, each tape being only a few minutes long (ninety bucks for THIS!!!). But I brought the tapes home and played them for Jacob and Molly, and we pointed along with the alphabet chart that went along with the first *ABC* song. I was amazed at the kids' response. Excitement! Retention! Let me do it again! My turn! Play the tape again! And much singing around the house of "A-A-APPLE, B-B-BALL, C-C-CAT, AND D-D-DOLL!!!" -- AND all this from Jacob yet, my least "sing-y" child, my child who rarely joined in at all when we sang as a family. That first day we decided to buy our own complete set, and it arrived in a week, and we haven't regretted spending that $90.00.

I decided not to start Jacob out with the first workbook, *Off We Go* (an introduction to each letter and its sound in alphabetical order), as I felt he already knew most individual sounds and was getting this all reviewed anyway with the first song in the set. He moved right into the second workbook and the games, and I began reading the little books aloud to Jacob and Molly, just as we'd read any new book aloud together. I decided not to keep the books unknown entities until the day when they were "supposed" to read them themselves.

I noticed a few things right off about the books. They were actual long stories (in numbers of pages) with rudimentary plots and amusing characters, even though they were built on an incredibly limited vocabulary. The first reader, the "Short A -- Apple Book" is 64 pages long (lots of page turning to really help you feel you are moving along fast), all with just short *A* words of 3 or 4 letters. And my kids thought it was funny, actually laughed out loud over the thing. And VERY quickly Jacob caught on to the before mysterious idea of sounding out words, completely new words -- what a breakthrough! Through the phonics songs, letter sounds are emphasized rather than letter names, so Jacob no longer had his old confusion about which in the world to use. He was launched.

Some "strict" phonics books are very strict about NO pictures -- a sort of paranoia that a child might (Heaven forbid!) get some clue to the story line from the pictures and therefore GUESS. *SSRW* does have pictures, plenty of them -- rather simple, even awkward illustrations, but at least they give some life to the stories, some humor and fun. It IS clear that the illustrations are "low budget." For instance, it's almost a guarantee that if a color word is mentioned in the text, the illustration will show it wrong -- the "brown shirt" is invariably blue or green. My kids weren't overly bothered by this and actually had fun pointing out these funny discrepancies, but I've heard some kids have been put off by it.

Jacob has not read through all of the books in the *SSRW* series, but just by our reading them aloud together he's gained a lot of useful phonics generalizations. It's not too hard to notice that the story focusing on the odd combination *KN* has *knights*, *knuckles*, *knit*, *knock*, *knew*, etc. Just the slightest bit of pointing this out while I am reading, asking Jacob or Molly to perhaps take a guess at the next *KN* word we come to, is often enough. They have the idea.

Also I found that once Jacob had a bit of experience in sounding out long vowel words, and had a working knowledge of most of the "letter clusters" like *OI, OY, SH, CH, TH, NG*, etc., he was ready to try out most of the REAL books we had in our home designed for beginning readers. Books like *Little Bear, Frog and Toad, Mr. Pine's Mixed-up Signs, The Cat in the Hat, Curious George Flies a Kite*, and simple versions of old folk tales. He didn't have to stay only with the *SSRW* books to the very end before realizing he could branch out with confidence to other things.

This reading of REAL books -- books with characters he'd already loved for years, warm and charming illustrations, quality binding -- was a tremendous boost and encouragement to Jacob. I think any family would be making a mistake to try to limit a child to ONLY the *SSRW* books -- though useful and fun, they are by no means great literature or beautiful books in themselves, and I think it would be unfair to a child to make him feel these were all he was "allowed" to read until he'd finished the whole set. Finding books a child LOVES is more important.

Sue Dickson continually reminds us that we need to help our kids have SUCCESS with beginning reading, not make them feel foolish, or feel they are being tested and quizzed relentlessly. And she realizes the value of a sense of humor and play -- very different from a phonics program I came across the other day that made it very clear that "the student is to have an attitude of WORK not PLAY." She is trying to make it easy for kids. Helpful mnemonic devices are all through the materials -- in the songs, in the jingles to help a child remember how to form a letter. What are often sterile "RULES" in most phonics approaches are here turned into amusing and memorable characters, like "Mr. *GH*" who usually "frightens" the vowels in a word into saying a different sound. And it's nice to be able to just hum a few bars of one of the phonics songs as a gentle way of reminding Jacob of how he might sound out a new word he's stuck on.

And even Hannah, at almost 3 months, beams out with big smiles if you sing the short vowel song to her during a diaper change, so I guess we ALL like it!

**Molly and Jacob Learn Phonics Together**

**Molly, beginning at age three, has been looking over Jacob's shoulder as he has been using *Sing, Spell, Read & Write*, and she has been learning phonics at the same time as Jacob. She is a little more passionate about words that don't fit the rules, ("Those bad rule breakers!") and a little slower in ability to combine sounds of letters in her head, but nevertheless, she has been learning. Susan wrote, when Molly was still three...**

As many of you have heard already via various grapevines (I almost thought about running the PENNSYLVANIA HOMESCHOOLERS PHONE TREE with the announcement...), we're expecting our fourth child in late summer. We're all starting to adjust happily to this surprise addition (and everyone here is looking forward to my SECOND trimester as opposed to my FIRST -- you know, hoping I'll peel myself off the sofa for a bit and get supper ready on time...) It seems like a fitting time to look over what it's like having three kids homeschooling and the values I've seen over the years for our kids in having siblings around all the time. May help me in making the adjustment to having FOUR homeschoolers in the family!!!

First there's the thought of what the younger ones learn from the older ones, and how special this is, and something that is hard to duplicate in schools. (Some schools do try to simulate the family, with elaborate programs of cross-age tutoring, but these relationships are certainly not as long term or special as having your own older brother and sister around every day...) I know Molly, now 3 1/2, would probably not be reading right now (yes, she can now read DICK AND JANE...) if she hadn't had Jacob's example to follow, if she hadn't had that overwhelming urge to DO WHAT HE DOES. Being a younger sister, she could tag along and listen-in in a very non-pressured way while I was helping Jacob, and pick up what she could for her own reasons. So she pretended to read for a long time, and gradually we all began realizing she could REALLY read.

And I think of Jacob always listening in on discussions really held with Jesse about various topics much to "hard" by any SCHOOL'S terms for a three, four, five, or six year old. Surprising what the little ones pick up. Jacob became as involved as Jesse in our last year's study of Civil War times, and gradually began adding his own ideas to our talks. Jacob knows all the funny stories about Lincoln, knows more about the Monitor and the Merrimac than I do, and can sing all the Civil War songs we learned. This year he still mentions things he picked up last year when he was the mere "younger tag-along" -- ideas really sunk in when I maybe thought he was just hanging on the fringes.

And vocabulary! The littler ones have picked up vocabulary from the older ones so easily -- not in any school-regimented workbook style way, but rather by always living with a world of words a bit above them. They overhear words like *octave*, or *improvise*, or *treble clef sign*, and they certainly don't know right off what they mean, and they don't question me about what they mean, but the words are there in the environment, and they know they have something to do with music and they gradually catch on. The words aren't introduced suddenly one day out of the blue by a music teacher in a third grade music class, but are old familiar friends that just become slowly more familiar and better known and understood. And how I loved to hear Molly importantly announce at age 3 that she was now going to "*improbise!*" on piano (therefore we should be quiet and listen respectfully).

Now I had perhaps expected all of these types of things to happen -- littler ones learning from bigger ones. It's very special

to watch unfold all around me, but not entirely a surprise --
seems like the natural sort of thing you would hope for with
homeschooling. But a thing that has really caught me off guard
is the fact that the littler ones in our family often inspire the
bigger ones. It has not been a one way street of older kids giving
and younger ones taking.

Take reading. As I said, Molly was certainly inspired by
Jacob in her strong drive to make sense of print. But he is
equally inspired by HER example. She does things to try to read
that Jacob has never thought of doing, and he takes some cues
from her and begins trying them too. One thing she does all the
time is to VERY carefully scan the print whenever I am reading
aloud to her -- something Jesse and Jacob NEVER did as pre-
readers. She suddenly calls out, "There's the word *look*" -- and
she's right! Or now she notices words that are ALMOST like
words she recognizes -- "That word is almost like *look*," and she
points and it's the word *book*. Or it becomes a game for them to
see who can call out a word I come to that I know they can
figure out.

We are now using the *Sing, Spell, Read & Write* program at
home, and having great fun with it. And again Molly inspires
Jacob, and Jacob inspires Jesse -- and Jesse inspires Jacob, and
Jacob inspires Molly, round and round again. Molly and Jacob
can play the simple Bingo-type game SOUND-O together very
happily (we always play cooperatively, not competitively!),
sometimes Jacob helping Molly find a letter on her card, and
sometimes Molly pointing out a letter to Jacob. And Molly was
the first of the two to feel confident enough to play the game
with lower case letters rather than upper case -- and Jacob
quickly followed suit. Jesse is going through the whole program
in order to help his spelling (it's his decision), and this has made
Jacob more eager to keep going and moving along. (Jacob is
right now officially "ahead" of Jesse, and therefore feels VERY
proud!) They ALL sing the phonics songs together, Jesse not
thinking its babyish, Molly not thinking it's too hard, Jacob
pleased to have everyone else part of what he's doing...

Informal Phonics Lessons

Many parents teach phonics at home without using a specific phonics series. Cindy Dale, for example, taught her two year old some phonics just by using an alphabet book. Cindy would say, "This is *A*." And Taraka would respond, "This is *A*." Each day they would go through this book, as it was one of Taraka's favorites. Eventually, Cindy began to ask, "What is this letter?" And Taraka would just naturally know the letter's name. Then Cindy told Taraka a sound for each letter in the same book, and soon she was asking Taraka, "What is this sound?" By the time Taraka was three, she could tell a sound for every letter. Taraka loved it. Soon Cindy was wondering if Taraka could put the sounds in words together and learn to read that way, but when she saw that it was too difficult for Taraka she dropped this attempt. She was watching Taraka for clues of readiness, and was in no hurry.

When Taraka was four and a half, Cindy was searching for a way to resume reading instruction. She found a book called *Teach Your Child to Read* by R. Baker Bausell, Carole R. Bausell & Nellie B. Bausell which suggested that parents teach their children the vowels. So, first Cindy told Taraka which letters were vowels and which were consonants. Then she began to teach each vowel separately. Taraka readily learned the short sound for each vowel. Then Cindy told Taraka rules for when a vowel would have its short sound and when it would have its long sound. Soon Taraka was sounding out words that her mother would write down. She would notice final silent *E's* and if two vowels were next to each other.

When Taraka was about five, she could look at a word and put it together. Soon she was reading a Walt Disney book about *Snow White* which she had enjoyed when it was read to her. Whenever she halted at a word that her mother didn't think she could sound out, her mother would tell her the word. Sometimes, when she halted at a word that could be sounded-out using a rule that Taraka knew, her mother would remind her about the rule ("What does that *E* at the end tell you?") and Taraka would be able to figure out the word.

Similarly, Willy Moffatt enjoyed learning how to sound out the vowels at age five. He already knew the sounds of the consonants -- he had learned them by playing games with magnetic letters on the refrigerator when his mother would be doing dishes. On a typical day he would pick out a letter and ask, "Mommy, what is the sound for this?" Judy would reply, "That *C* makes the 'cuh' sound." Sometimes she'd start a game, "Let's think of all the words in the kitchen that start with *C*." And they'd come up with *cup*, *cupboard*, and *cookies*. Then Willy might say, "Let's think of all the words in the park that start with *C*." This pleasant game would go on until the dishes were done, a perfect example of informal teaching and companionship!

At about the same time, Judy would often read to Willy from a Richard Scary alphabet book. Willy had his favorite pages which they would read hundreds of times. At first, Willy would point to a picture and ask, "What is this?" Judy would say the word underneath the picture and underline it when she'd say it. After they had read the page together many times, Willy would sometimes try it himself. He would underline a word with his finger and say the word while he was moving his finger from left to right. One of his favorite words was *oom-pa-pa*, which was written by a picture of a pig playing a trombone.

One night, Judy was paying the bills while Willy was sleeping in his room next to the kitchen. Willy, never a heavy sleeper, came into the kitchen and found his mother muttering, "How could they possibly want this much for the telephone?" Willy crawled up on her lap and wanted to know what she was doing. Judy explained that she was looking over the telephone bill and she showed him it, "Look, there's the time the call was made, there's the date, and there's the place that the call was made to." Then Willy asked about the words *date*, *time*, and *place* written across the top of the page. First he asked, "Which word means the time?" Then he wanted to know how she knew that *date* said "date" and *place* said "place." "How do you know that *place* doesn't say 'date'?"

Judy slowly sounded-out the word *date* and said, "Remember those games we play with the magnetic letters when we start with the *D* sound?" Then he wanted to know why the *A* made the "long-*A*" sound not the "short-*A*" sound. Judy pointed out the *E* at the end and said that when a vowel is alone between two consonants and there is an *E* at the end of the word, then that vowel makes the long sound. Willy asked, "Why?" and Judy explained that that was the way it was, and she wasn't sure why.

Then Willy sounded out the word *time* by himself and he got very excited. Then he read *place* and he read all three words over and over. Then he asked his mother to write other words so that he could read them. She put *lake*, *bake*, and *cake* on cards and he read them and soon was jumping up and down and hugging his mother. After that he wanted to read everything. They'd be driving and he'd read words on posters and signs, and he was always asking about the rules behind how words were spelled.

Soon his mother showed him the *OA* in words like *boat* and *coat*. Willy asked, "Why isn't it spelled *BOTE*? Is someone trying to trick me?" Although he didn't like the inconsistency of English spelling, he did go on to read more and more, and soon became a fine reader.

### Discovering Phonics Ideas as an Adult

Someone once asked me whether I thought it was important for already fluent readers to go back and learn phonics. I said, "No. The purpose of phonics is to help you learn to read. The only reason to learn phonics once you can read, is so that you can help others learn to read." Susan has been learning phonics lately. She writes...

One thing that has been fun for me as an adult trying to help my kids make sense of print and the patterns of our language, is that I've come to understand some phonics or spelling patterns that I've never seen written about in books. I've been doing some of my own detective work now, and it's exciting to pass this on to the kids. Take the words *have* and *live*. They seem to be "rulebreakers" because of the short sound of the first vowel even though there is an *E* at the end of the word (a usual signal for a long vowel sound). But when I began thinking about it I suddenly realized that in English, we NEVER have a word end in a plain un-adorned *V*. *V* just always takes an *E* after it at the end of a word -- that's its pattern in our language. Other languages are different (I think of the *Kirov Ballet...*), but that's just the way English is.

Also it's been fascinating to gradually discover the various nationality roots of strange word families in English. Ours is indeed a "melting pot" language, taking words from all over the place. For instance, we'd found that *CH* could make one of three sounds -- most commonly the one in *choo-choo*, but also the *SH* sound found in *chandelier* or *Chicago*, or the *K* sound as in *Christmas* or *chorus* or *school*. It was comforting to me to read that the odd *SH* sounding *CH* words are most usually from French, and the *K* sounding *CH* words are from Greek. A quick look through a good dictionary that gives word origins confirms this. Indeed I can imagine an older child getting quite excited to discover these sorts of generalizations using a quality dictionary. I'm not saying a six year old should be required to remember this of course, but I think some knowledge of word origins CAN help a child realize that there IS a consistency to our language, it's just that our language's roots are so complex and tangled that things sometimes seem more arbitrary than they are. And more importantly, perhaps seeing a parent or other adult actively trying to ferret out these consistencies or patterns, finding meaning in seemingly chaotic "messes" is a good model for our kids (AND I just looked it up in the dictionary, and *chaos* IS a Greek word...). Also it shows once again that the study of anything can bring you to everywhere -- studying even phonics and spelling patterns can bring in the whole flow of Western history.

# 5. Helping Children Learn to Read

Sometimes, when we're sitting around a campfire, I tell my kids some made-up stories about our monkey puppet (named "Monkey") and his friend John going camping. Generally, one of the trouble spots comes when they try to build a fire. Sometimes John just gets the fire sparked and started when Monkey brings over a whole pile of leaves (which he thought would burn) and drops them upon the fire smothering it out.

Part of building a campfire is sparking it with a match. The other part is gently kindling it little by little until it becomes a roaring blaze. If little sticks are not continually added the fire will die out, if the sticks that are added are too big, they may not catch, and too much at once is sure to smother the flame.

This chapter consists of stories of parents who have helped their children learn to read much as a woodsman might kindle a campfire. Sometimes these parents have helped to spark their children's interest. Sometimes they have carefully nurtured the fire until it finally grew into a roaring flame. Above all, these parents did not smother the fire but instead fed it little by little until their children finally became fluent readers.

Brian Teaches Himself to Read

Brian Coughenour taught himself to read. He had always been the kind of child who would figure things out on his own. When he was a baby he would do much of his babbling when lying by himself after waking up from a nap. He was also the kind of child who treasured his favorite stories and liked to hear them over and over again.

Like almost all home-schooled children, he was read to from an early age. He would listen to his favorite stories again and again until he practically had them memorized. He learned the alphabet after having an alphabet book read to him many times. When he was three, his parents found him off by himself reading his favorite book. Actually he had memorized it -- he knew the words by where they were on the page. When his mother would be reading to him, he would be looking closely at the words. Once, he pointed out to her that she was turning the page before speaking the words at the bottom.

When watching Sesame Street on TV, he would see words put together ($F + AKE = FAKE$; $L + AKE = LAKE$). He became interested in how sounds and letters are related and he began to question why some words are not as they "should" be. At about age four and a half, or perhaps five, he began to read books which had not been previously read to him. By the time he turned six, he would frequently read on his own although he still enjoyed being read to.

Brian taught himself to read by reading books which he had memorized. His reading stemmed from his loving books so much that he wanted to hear them, or read them, again and again. He once asked his mother, "Wouldn't it be a terrible world if you could only read a book once?"

When people ask Debbye Coughenour how she taught Brian to read, she responds that he taught himself. While he did teach himself, that's only part of the story. She read stories to him as often as he wanted to hear them, bought books that he could treasure, and put his books on a low shelf where he could get them whenever he wanted.

There is a certain similarity between how some homeschooled children "teach themselves" to read and the way some children "teach themselves" to use a potty. I was over at a home-schooling family's house when it hit me. Kate McPherson had just mentioned that her littlest one had just taught herself to use a toilet, and I realized that my little daughter Molly had also just taught herself. Generally, in our society, most children are toilet *trained* and *taught* to read. One method of toilet training is to put children on toilets and force them to stay there until they use it.

When Molly taught herself to use a potty, we put the potty at floor level. She was allowed to walk around naked so that she could easily use it. She was allowed in the bathroom to see her family use the toilet. Every time she said, "Pee!" somebody accompanied her to the bathroom (and quickly!). When she did pee in the toilet or potty she had an appreciative audience noting her accomplishment.

In general, children who teach themselves to read all share some common home conditions: (1) their interest in words and print is encouraged by their parents, (2) their parents are willing to read books to them over and over until they have the books memorized, (3) the books are kept at a height where they can get them out on their own whenever they want, (4) they have an appreciative audience who listens to them read and notes their accomplishments.

### Bobby Learns to Read by Memorizing Words

Bobby McMonigal has always had an excellent memory. When he was four he became interested in the words his mother, Gerry, was reading to him. Sometimes he would point to a word and ask Gerry what it was. After she'd tell him, he'd repeat the word and he would learn it. Then he asked Gerry to underline the words with her finger while she read. When she came to a word that he did not know, he would stop her finger and thus halt her reading while he studied the word. Through such study, he began to build up a large reading vocabulary.

When Bobby was four and a half, he got a book off a library shelf and found that because he knew so many words, he could read it. When he came to a word that he did not know, his mother simply told him what it was. He read many books this way.

When he was almost six and already a pretty good reader, his mother purchased a phonics workbook. She thought that Bobby would be able to read better if he knew about long and short vowels. When she tried to use the workbook with Bobby, he got upset. After a while, he wouldn't even look at the page. Despite his exceptional reading, he couldn't seem to hear the differences between the different vowel sounds.

Apparently, children can learn to read without ever learning the difference between a "short-*E*" sound and a "short-*I*" sound. I have been studying Hebrew and have noticed that many of the vowel sounds are written below the letters for the beginning reader but are dropped in the newspapers and in most books. Fluent readers of Hebrew do not need to see these vowels in order to read the words. Perhaps children like Bobby discover on their own what very few adults realize -- that in English, like Hebrew, in the flow of context, words can be distinguished from each other without paying much attention to the sounds of the vowels.

Emily Learns to Read at Age Two

With some children the fire is easily kindled. When Madalene and Tom Murphy's eldest, Emily, was just two and a half, she loved to have the same books read to her over and over again. *The Ginger Bread Man* and *Small Pig* were her favorites. She must have listened to *Small Pig* hundreds of times. Emily didn't pay much attention to pictures, but she did pay attention to words. Soon she demanded that her mother underline the words with her finger when reading so that Emily could follow along. Soon Madalene and Emily started to play a game. After Madalene would finish reading a page, she would point to a word on the page for Emily to read.  Emily loved the game.  Sometimes, after they had finished reading together, Emily would take the book off by herself.  One day, her parents found her sitting on her bed reading *The Little Engine That Could* to herself.  By the time Emily was three, she was a reader.

## Christian Learns the Same Way

While Emily looked at the words more than the pictures when her parents were reading, her little brother, Christian, looked at the pictures, and he really did notice what was in the pictures!  For example, when his parents were reading him a book in which a bulldozer knocked down a statue and dragged it away, Christian noticed that when the bulldozer knocked down the statue, the illustration showed that the statue's feet were left on the base.  Six pages later, he noticed that when people were on the statue while it was being pulled by the bulldozer, the feet were shown as if they were still attached to the statue.  "Hey, wait a second!" he said.  Then he flipped back to the earlier illustration and pointed out the discrepancy.

While Emily liked books to be read over and over to her, Christian quickly got bored with a simple book.  Where Emily at the same age would have wanted to listen to a simple *Babar* book, Christian would want to hear a heavy *Narnia* book.  He wasn't at all interested in the kind of books that he would have been reading if he were beginning to read.

One day, when Christian was about five and a half, his mother decided to try to teach him to read the same way that Emily had learned.  She got out the book, *Small Pig*, which had been Emily's favorite, and she read it to him several times.  Then, after she'd read a page, she asked Christian, "Do you want to find *pig* for me?"  While this game had been enthusiastically received by two year old Emily, five year old Christian was not at all enthusiastic.  He would only tolerate *Small Pig* for a little while before he would want to listen to something more interesting.  Nevertheless, after several sessions with *Small Pig*, Christian had it memorized and he could read it aloud. His parents were not sure, however, if he was really reading it, or just repeating it from memory. At that point, reading instruction was dropped for about six months.

The real breakthrough came when Christian was six. He found an easy to read book at a book sale called *Look Out For Pirates* which he bought with 10 cents of his own money. The book had nice pictures, and an interesting story line, large print, and not too many words on a page. For the first time, he was interested in listening to a book being read over and over again. Perhaps he had learned, through his experience with *Small Pig* that he could learn to read by listening to a book frequently and then matching the written and spoken words.

That week his mother and father each read *Look Out For Pirates* to him a few times. Tom, his father, read it in a very funny manner making fun of the language spoken by the characters, because, as in other easy reading books, the characters just don't talk normally. Christian liked the way his father read it. Soon, he was off by himself matching the words on the page to the story as he knew it.

Then he was able to read it aloud, and it wasn't that he simply had it memorized. He was so into it, that he dramatized it on cassette tape and started writing down the whole book in order to make a "new" book.

Next, Madalene tried a phonics workbook with him. Christian didn't like the "stories" in the workbook. One day he looked up and said, "This is really boring!" His mother agreed, and so the workbook was put away.

Instead, they started using library books and easy reading books they had around. Madalene or Tom would listen to him read each day. One day, when he was about six and a half, he was looking at a tool catalogue, making plans for a current woodworking project. No one was available to read the captions to him, so he decided to read them to himself.

When he came to a word he didn't understand, he'd ask somebody about it, spelling it out loud. Soon he had bookmarks placed throughout the catalog so that he could ask about all of the unknown words the next time a parent would be available.

By age eight, Christian became a good enough reader to read the kind of fiction books to himself that he enjoyed. On a typical night, his father might first read to him from *Touchstone* by Robert Louis Stevenson and then say "good night." Then Christian might read from *Star of Wild Horse Canyon* before turning out the light.

Emily and Christian learned at different ages, yet both now are fluent readers. They both learned to read by listening to stories over and over again, and then by paying the attention necessary to match the words on the page with the stories as they remembered them.

The Murphys have invented a new reading method that is particularly suited for homeschoolers. It doesn't use reading textbooks or phonics workbooks, it just uses books you find around the house, or buy at yard sales, or get out of libraries. You start by getting cozy and reading a favorite book out loud. After you have read the book upteen times, you start playing the game. It works with two year olds like Emily and five year olds like Christian. The principle of the method is -- "ignite the fire and nurture it."

### Felicity Gets Inspired by a Gift

Felicity Newell's interest in reading was sparked by a gift. There is a slogan, "Never underestimate the power of a woman!" I think a similarly true slogan would be, "Never underestimate the power of something new!"

Felicity Newell had learned the alphabet and the sounds of the letters when she was six. Her mother, Ruth, had put word labels all around the house and words on word cards including every word from the Dr. Seuss book, *Hop on Pop*. But Felicity had dragged her feet, and reading instruction had been suspended for a while.

Then, when Felicity was just about seven, her grandmother sent her a set of reading text books about a fictional English community. Felicity took to the books right away. Each book built upon the last book, and the series developed the characters and the setting. In some ways the series perfectly fit the Newells. Ruth is English and they have always been interested in England.

Soon after the books arrived, her mother came down with the flu, and Felicity brought the books to the bedroom in order to "read" them to her mother. After all, she knew her mother read to her when she was sick. That began formal reading instruction again.

For the next several months, Felicity stayed with the first few books in the series. She would read them to her mother and to her little sister. Also, she and her little sister incorporated the characters in the books into their imaginative play. They had little figures which they pretended were the people in the reader.

Felicity read the first readers so often that soon it wasn't clear whether she was reading them, or repeating them from memory. Although she could read those particular books, she still did not consider herself a reader. She wanted to be able to read the *Narnia* books by C. S. Lewis, which she had enjoyed listening to so much. When she was almost seven and a half she would still state that she did not like reading.

Suddenly, when she was seven and a half, things took off. She had been making slow but steady progress in the reading series. She had just finished reviewing the earlier books in the series by working through some workbooks which Grandmother had belatedly sent along. Perhaps the review helped her, perhaps the writing in the workbooks helped. Whatever the reason, she took off.

She began to read picture books which had earlier been read to her. She even read and enjoyed *Hop on Pop* which she had earlier disliked. Three months later she was reading long books with several chapters, and had even begun reading the *Narnia* series to herself. A couple of years later, Felicity had become such a fluent reader that she was able to read *Wuthering Heights* to herself. She and her mother each read it so that they could discuss it with each other. I know that I did not read *Wuthering Heights* until I was a senior in High School, and I had a difficult time with it then.

### Jesse Begins to Read to Himself

When Jesse first started silently reading to himself, there were still many words that he did not know. He found that, when reading silently, he could skip words that he did not know and still get the gist of what he was reading. The first long chapter book that Jesse read was a book about Robin Hood. Jesse finished one chapter and told us he had just read "Robin Hood and the Butterchurn." Susan didn't think that there was a chapter in the book with that name and found that Jesse had really just finished "Robin Hood and the Butcher!" The point is that Jesse was not reading every word correctly, but he continued to read silently, and this is the way he became a fluent reader.

Jesse has always been a social reader -- in other words he has always seen reading as part of the social situation of being read to or reading to someone. All through his learning to read, he never was one to take books off by himself. In order to encourage Jesse to read to himself a little each day, Susan made it a social situation.

For at least a month, Jesse would read silently to himself while Susan would sit near him reading to herself *and* nursing or holding a napping Molly, and Jacob would look through books silently to himself. Susan made it a point to read adult books SHE was interested in for herself -- NOT books for the kids, or books about homeschooling! They actually set a kitchen timer for fifteen minutes at first, and even took the phone off the hook to help concentration. After the timer sounded, they'd talk informally with each other about what they'd been reading. After that month of "social" silent reading, Jesse was hooked, and would read silently to himself while the others would be in another room doing something else. (Maybe toddler Molly helped the transition by not continuing to be very silent herself!)

To encourage Jesse, Susan asked him to put the titles of any chapters or books that he'd read on cards. These were taped to the wall along our stairway, forming Jesse's first "Stairway of Books." When Jesse had read enough to fill the stairway (one for each step), we had a little ceremony while Jesse stapled the titles together to make a little book. When Jesse was seven, Susan wrote...

As Jesse began reading more and more books on his own this year, I wanted him to begin taking responsibility for keeping track of books completed -- thought it would save me a bit of record keeping. I felt it was important to show a full listing of Jesse's independent reading when I met with our assistant superintendent, as we don't use any reading "series," and so can't describe his progress in "levels." I first suggested Jesse write titles of books completed in a stapled together notebook. Jesse perfunctorily wrote titles down a few times, if reminded, but clearly had no interest in the ritual, and usually managed to misplace his "Book's Book." It was just another idea that petered out. Once in our new house another idea came to me. I saw the woodwork along our stairway in a new way -- couldn't Jesse display cards along it, showing what books he'd read? He could see his "stairway of books" grow every day. The idea had instant appeal to Jesse. We decided that new books he'd never read before would be one color card, and old favorites that he was rereading would be another color.

At first, Jesse reread lots of well known easy books, but very soon began trying more and more new books. As he said, "you can TELL the difference now." We held a bit of a ceremony when Jesse completed his first stairway -- Jesse read aloud all the titles from bottom to top, then with great pomp untaped them and flew them down to me at the bottom of the stairs, and then we stapled them together and put a little cover on it all. Jesse's now on his fifth "stairway," and the idea hasn't gotten old yet.

I'd always shied away from ideas like this before, feeling they were too close to the gimmicky "bookworms" strung across school bulletin boards, where competition and quantity become more important than enjoying reading. At home, though, there's no extrinsic competition involved, no time limits beyond the goals Jesse might set for himself. For Jesse at age 7, the idea is just a lot more concrete and visual -- and fun -- than merely recording titles in a booklet. AND Jesse doesn't need reminding about it (usually!), AND our superintendent was impressed. I'm pleased!

### Julie Reads When Her Mother Can't

One home-schooled child, Julie Schlereth, took off into reading when she realized that her mother would soon be undergoing a jaw operation and there would be several months where she would not be able to enjoy books unless she read them to herself.

Like other homeschoolers, Julie had always enjoyed hearing her mother read aloud. Even when nursing, reading aloud would soothe her. She talked and walked early. By the time she was four, she could sing the alphabet song, point out the letters of the alphabet, and could write her name. Beginning at age five, she had been writing letters to her Aunt. When she didn't know a word she would ask her mother how to spell it. However, she couldn't or wouldn't read any books herself.

When she was just six years old, she would play a word card game with her mother. Her mother wrote down all the words on cards that Julie knew. Then they started to make sentences using the words. Sometimes Julie would ask for a word to be put on a card because she needed it in a sentence.

When Julie was six and a half, her mother began to work with her using the McGuffey readers. They got up to lesson 5, and then Julie refused to go on. Her mother said, "Today we must do something. Let's read your McGuffey reader." Julie replied, "I hate those books. I'm going to throw them away."

I have heard similar stories from other home-schooling parents. The general pattern is that a child starts reading at the beginning of a first grade reading text book and keeps reading on a daily basis until the stories get frustrating, and then reading instruction ends for a while. I made the same mistake once myself. I was tutoring a 10 year old school-educated boy who could not read. I started having him read a little each day from a beginning reader, but the book soon got too difficult and he got frustrated.

I failed to realize that when schools use textbooks they teach each five or six page chapter for a whole week. The children study the words in isolation, do worksheets, read, and reread. I was doing a chapter a day instead of a chapter a week. The solution is simple. Either home-schooled parents have to imitate the schools and slow down, or they have to use several beginning readers at once, going from one to the other so as to stay at an easy level for a much longer time. When Jacob was beginning with "Dick and Jane," we had several editions of those readers and so he was able to go back and forth between them. Getting back to Julie Schlereth...

When she was six and three quarters she read her first book. It was just before Christmas and she read a very simple book, *The Christmas Santa Almost Missed* by Marion Francis. It was about Santa losing his cap and not being able to find it. She also read a *Sesame Street* book that she had listened to at least a hundred times. In January she read another book by Marion Francis, *Who Cried for Pie*. Despite these successes, she still did not consider herself a reader. As she approached seven, when her mother would say, "Let's read," she would say, "No way!"

There is a curious stage in children's progress into reading when they appear to have all the elements together that they need, but they still aren't reading. They may know lots of words, but something about all those words on a page in a book scares them. Julie was at this stage for several months. Then, as she turned seven, something happened -- her mother got TMJ, a serious jaw dysfunction which made it difficult for her to talk (or read out loud!) and Julie began to hear about the operation that would result in her mother's jaw being temporarily wired shut.

Soon, in response to an appeal in our homeschooling newsletter, other homeschooling families began to send tapes of their reading aloud to the Schlereths. Some of those families' recordings included children reading aloud. After hearing the children, Julie decided to make a tape of herself reading *A Kiss for Little Bear*, a book that she had practically memorized. One day, Julie's mother found her slowly reading a book that she had listened to hundreds of times. She came to the word, *Madeline* that she must have known from context and her mother saw her sounding it out. Her mother wondered why Julie was sounding out words that she already knew, or at least could easily guess from context. I think she was looking closely at the words and noting how the sounds fit with the letters.

Soon Julie started to like to read. Just after she turned seven she was talking to her Grandmother on the telephone and said, "Grandma, when I come over, I'm going to bring a book to read to you!" By the time Patty had her operation, Julie was a reader.

### Anita Learns to Read at Age Twelve

Many home-schooled children of the past did not learn to read until they were ten or twelve, yet this late start did not prevent them from eventually becoming excellent readers. Two notable examples, General George Patton and President Woodrow Wilson, did not learn to read until shortly before entering high school. During World War II Patton read the book on tank warfare by the German General Erwin Rommel and effectively used those tactics against the Germans. Wilson wrote history books and great speeches. He is the only President of the United States to have obtained a doctoral degree.

Even today there are a few cases of home-educated children who do not learn to read until they are ten or twelve. Although Anita Giesy had learned the letters and some phonics at an earlier age, she did not start to read seriously until she was ten and did not take-off into reading until she was twelve.

When Anita was ten, she told her mother that she wanted to learn to read menus at restaurants. So she and her mother began to set aside some time each day when Anita would read aloud.

First Anita read *Meet Theodore Roosevelt* by Ormonde DeKay Jr, a "Step-up" biography with about 86 pages filled with large- type words. At the beginning, she would read about a page a day, but by the end she was reading an entire three page chapter in a day. Whenever she would come to a word that she didn't know, her mother would tell her whether that word followed the rules or not. For example, if it was a word like "laugh" Theo would say, "That word doesn't sound out, if you don't know it, you're not going to be able to figure it out." However, when Anita would stop at a word that followed the rules Theo would say, "That can be sounded out." Then Anita would approach the word on her own if she wanted to. Every sentence was an effort. She'd have to read it several times. The first reading of a sentence would be to figure out what the words were, and the second reading would be to figure out the meaning. Anita complained that she didn't like to read because she couldn't get pictures in her mind of what was going on.

Meanwhile, Theo was continuing to read to both her and her older sister Susie. Reading together had long been a shared and valued experience in the Giesy household. Usually they would read in bed just before the girls would go to sleep. One night, Theo started drifting off to sleep in the middle of a sentence, and Anita woke her up and pointed to and read the next few words to get Theo going again. Anita was obviously looking at the words while her mother was reading.

When Anita was eleven she started babysitting. She had always enjoyed being read to so she decided to take books to read to the child she was sitting for. One time she read five of her books to the child. Whenever she'd babysit she'd read books out loud and in this real situation she read more than she had ever read before.

Soon, she started reading silently to herself at home and she could get the pictures in her mind which allowed her to enjoy what she read. For example, she'd be reading about walking through a snowy street and she'd be able to see the lane and the shops on either side. Soon Anita's good friend Ellie read her the first few chapters of a teenage romance written at about a sixth grade reading level. Anita continued reading it to herself at her own pace, about two pages per day. Typically, Anita would be lying on her bed reading to herself while her mother would be nearby sewing. When Anita wouldn't know a word she would spell it out loud and her mother would call back the word.

Anita continued to progress with reading, and she also got into writing. When I saw her a few years later, she showed me the first sixty pages of a novel that she was writing.

Nathan Gets to the Top of the Mountain

For some children learning to read is like a long climb up a tall mountain. When Nathan Wilcox was seven and a half, I gave him a reading test which his parents and I hoped could demonstrate to their school superintendent that Nathan was indeed learning to read.

Nathan had been reading for about ten months. He had learned the alphabet; he had learned about long vowel sounds and silent *E's* at the end of words. He had been reading a little almost every day for the past ten months and he was just beginning to read easy books himself. His current project was Dr. Seuss's *The Cat In the Hat*, which he was reading two or three pages a day. Despite all this reading, when I gave him the reading test he only scored at the same level as the average child beginning first grade, so, according to the test, Nathan had not yet begun to read.

Nevertheless, Nathan's parents were optimistic. His father said, "I think he'll make it next year. He's at the point where he's beginning to desire the information that books offer. Until children get a little good at it, reading is not exactly great fun. It takes a little effort. It's not so different from many other things in life. Many things take effort before we get to enjoy them."

About eight months later, Nathan read a simple book called *Mr. Cuckoo's Clock Shop*, to his infant sister, Autumn. After he put that away he picked up *The Case of the Hungry Stranger*, an *I Can Read Mystery* by Crosby Bonsall. Noticing him browsing through this library book, his mother said to him, "It really won't be long before you'll be able to read this book. You already know most of these words."

Nathan liked mysteries, so he looked through the book. But it looked too hard -- he sneered, "Oh yeah, right!" and slammed the book shut and threw it on the shelf. But about a half hour later his parents found him sitting on the couch with his legs propped up looking at the mystery book. He was reading silently and chuckling to himself! First he got the page down so that he knew it, and then he'd read it out loud. His mother called out from the kitchen, "Nathan, is that you over there reading that page?"

Nathan read that page and another page, and in one sitting he read seventeen pages. First he would read to himself a little bit, then he would read to his parents. For the first time he seemed to be able to sound-out long words. He seemed to be looking closely at the first few letters and then guessing the word. Since he was reading with understanding, there were only a few possibilities that each word could be. Sometimes he couldn't get it, then he would spell it out and his parents would tell him what it was. He finished that book in two more days and then began to get other *I Can Read Mysteries* like *The Case of the Cat's Meow* from the library.

A few months later, his parents told me about their excitement that day. His mother said, "I loved to see him sitting over there silently reading and laughing. Seeing that happen really made me feel that homeschooling was all right. Now he reads for enjoyment when he reads. I know he's going to enjoy reading."

His father added, "Children have got to learn that they can take off in many areas of life and reading is one of the first examples of it -- something which seemed like a mountain they had to climb and all of a sudden they got to the top and they soared out beyond it and a new horizon opened up."

Later that day I gave Nathan the same reading test that he had taken eleven months earlier and found that he had gone up about two and a half years in reading level.

After the test I asked Nathan if he had any advice for others. "I know a couple of kids," I said, "who can't read yet and their mothers are really worried because they're afraid that their kids aren't going to learn to read. Do you have anything to say to those mothers?"

He answered, "Don't worry, in time they will want to read. Like one day they may pick up a book and discover that it isn't boring, it's fun!"

"Do you have anything to say to kids who can't read yet and might be worried that they might not ever be able to read?"

"Always have faith," Nathan replied, "because you *will* learn to read!"

INTRODUCTION TO OUR BOOK, THE ANIMALS OF RICHMAN FARM

INTRODUCTION    by Jesse Richman

THE ANIMALS OF RICHMAN FARM is lots of little
stories put together in one book.  All of the
stories are true, with exciting adventures of cats,
dogs, goats, goldfish, and insects, with little and
big illustrations.  The illustrations which are
whiteness on a black background are prints, so are
the pictures which are often really thick lines.
Neither of the prints are woodblocks. The white on
black background ones are done on styrofoam, and the
others are rubber glued on to old bookcovers or
wood.

Hope you enjoy the book!

# 6. First Steps Toward Writing

Some children begin to write even before they can read. One successful educator, Maria Montessori, even taught writing before reading. After she had taught her students the one-to-one letter-to-sound correspondences of the Italian language, Montessori would get them started with writing words by sounding them out. Her students would get excited as they suddenly discovered that they could write any words they could speak and then read the words that they had just written.

Unfortunately, English is not as phonetic a language as Italian. In order to get one-to-one correspondences in English for the beginning writer-reader to use, the English alphabet has to be bent a little. One of the most successful English-language school reading programs of all time used ITA, an artificial alphabet which closely resembled the regular alphabet except that there was one sound for each letter and one letter for each sound -- 44 symbols in all. ITA was never dropped because of bad results -- every study found that children who learned with ITA became better readers faster than children who learned with the regular alphabet. And interestingly, the children not only learned to read, they also learned to write.

I have talked with teachers who had taught first grade classes using ITA. They all talked nostalgically of how even these young children would write up a storm. Sometimes the teachers would fish through their file cabinets and pull out the odd spellings and the fun stories that their pupils came up with.

ITA was dropped for several reasons. First it meant that schools would have had to buy libraries of books written in a different alphabet for their first graders to read. Second, ITA's text-book was being published by an independent publisher, and the big-time publishers who had big-name reading specialists under contract were losing some of the reading textbook market. Finally, one study found that a good reading program which used sound-spelling writing with the regular alphabet could get the same excellent results as those obtained with ITA...[12] Unfortunately, when ITA was dropped, sound-spelling writing in first grade was also dropped.

There is a new program sponsored by IBM called *Write to Read* which fills the Kindergarten classroom with IBM typewriters and computers and encourages children to engage in sound-spelling. Unfortunately, it is designed for use in Kindergarten, rather than First Grade and forms part of the movement to bring formal instruction to ever-younger children. Nevertheless, it may herald the beginning of a revival of sound-spelling in the schools.

## Jesse Begins Sound-Spelling

When Jesse was about six and able to recognize all the letters and about sixty words, he was quite reluctant to do sound-spelling writing. He always wanted to spell every word that he wrote correctly. The result was rather stilted sentences which always contained the same words.

At about that time, I found a book in the library called, *How They Murdered the Second "R"* and Susan and I read about the use of ITA sound-spelling in the schools. The author included several examples of the delightful writing of first grade children when they were encouraged to spell words any way that they could.

One day, I showed our monkey puppet (with Jesse watching) how he could use sound-spelling to make the vowel sounds. I made a chart showing Monkey how he could use

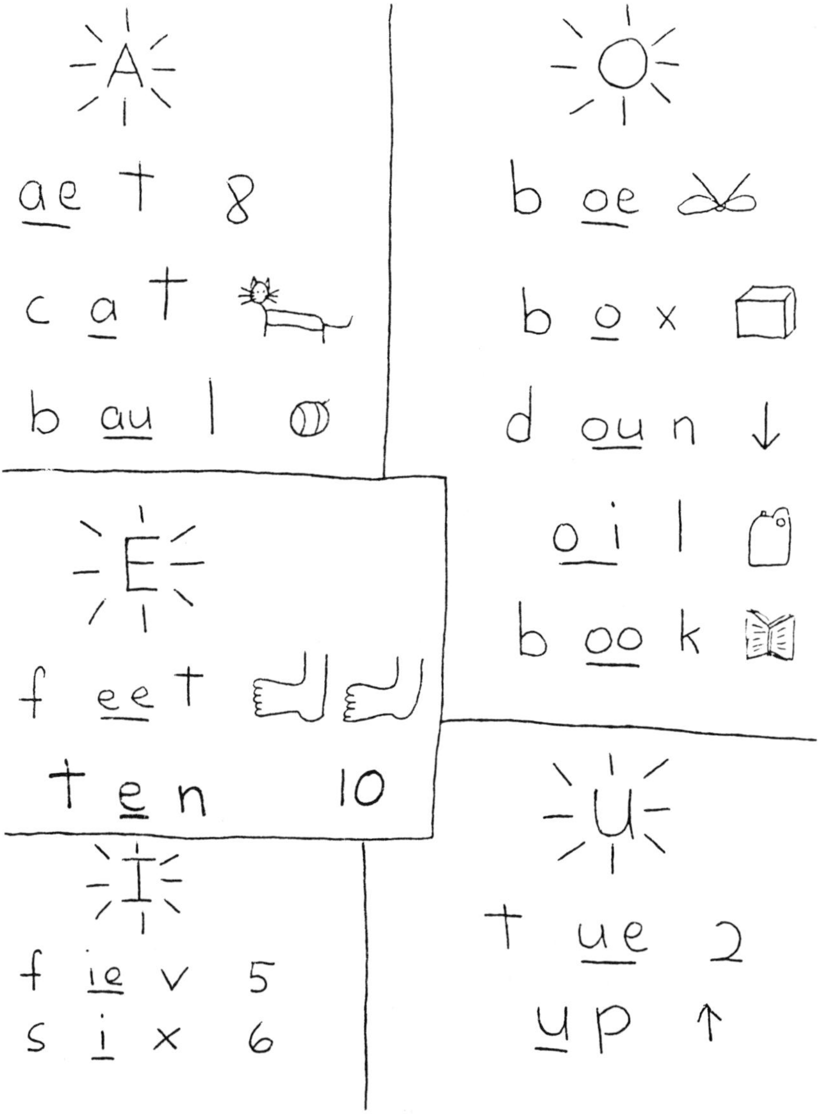

A (sun rays)

a‗e t 8

c a‗ t (cat)

b au‗ l (ball)

E (sun rays)

f ee‗ t (feet)

t e‗ n 10

I (sun rays)

f ie‗ v 5

s i‗ x 6

O (sun)

b oe‗ (bow)

b o‗ x (box)

d ou‗ n ↓

o‗ i l (oil can)

b oo‗ k (book)

U (sun rays)

t ue‗ 2

u‗ p ↑

any vowel followed by an "E" to make the long vowel sound, use the vowel by itself to make the short vowel sound, and use "OU," "OO," and "AU" to make some of the other sounds that occur.   It was a simple chart incorporating pictures and words that illustrated each sound.   Monkey liked the idea, and Jesse was interested.

Jesse asked me to write down the sound-spelling versions of some of the words that he already knew how to spell. He could see that the words usually looked about the same no matter which spelling was used -- "monkey" became "munkee," "ate" became "aet," "pie" stayed "pie" -- and he was sold.

Soon Jesse and our monkey puppet were writing sound-spelling stories back and forth and Jesse began to free up in his writing.  Around the same time, Susan began listening to Jesse read for about five minutes every night just before Susan would read the going-to-bed stories.   When Jesse didn't know a word, Susan would encourage him to sound it out and he progressed steadily as a reader. He has continued to both read and write, and now at age ten he is both a fluent reader and a lucid writer.  But the story of Jesse becoming a writer is really Susan's to tell.  When Jesse was almost seven, Susan wrote...

Over the past half year, Jesse has become a writer. He'd been dictating stories, letters, and little poems for years, but he had no idea of how to even begin to do the actual work of translating his own spoken ideas into print himself.  Even forming letters was slow, exacting work.  For him to have written out his own pieces then would have been akin to us, as adults, having to carve our words in marble, with dull chisels at that -- a pretty arduous task. Jesse dabbled some with our electric typewriter, enjoying pretending to be typing fast, enjoying typing small parts of letters he'd dictated to his "Mother/Scribe" (i.e. *me*).  He was completely dependent, though, on copying my written out correct spellings of words he needed.  Early on, he wanted his spellings to be *right*.  I'd read in *Growing Without Schooling*

magazine about children happily "sound-spelling" when they
began to write on their own, and wondered if Jesse would ever
take off in this way.    I thought for a good while that his
temperament was just averse to the idea.    That has now all
changed.

A bit of chronology may help put this growing in
perspective...    In September, '83, we began a few small
"routines" that proved helpful and eventually led up to sound-
spelling.  Jesse and I decided that he would write out the whole
alphabet each month, upper and lower case, for display in our
livingroom.    He understood that we'd be keeping these
handwriting samples in our portfolio of work that we show to
our school district periodically.

September's alphabet was a tortuous affair.    Jesse hadn't
written much over the summer, and his letters were wobbly,
awkward, uncomfortable for him to form.  He was also severely
critical of his work, would cut out any "wrong" letters and tape
on a new piece of paper -- the whole alphabet was a twisting
segmented crumple.  He kept at the job though -- the task had
become self-chosen.    Then, sometime that month, Jesse was
hanging about the kitchen table while I was cooking supper.  I
laid down a sheet of blank paper and suggested that he write
something, anything at all, just write. He began, and by the time
the stew was ready to serve, he'd proudly written out several
lines of wobbly print. He wrote only disconnected words, "safe"

words that he was sure he knew how to spell (Mommy, Daddy, etc...). From that night on, he wrote almost daily and I felt progress was happening. He was growing physically more comfortable with pencil and paper, he was writing out lots *more* each day, he seemed pleased with what he was doing.

Oddly, he decided that he would just keep *re*writing what he'd written the day before, maybe adding a new line, even slowly beginning to put his separate words into little sentences ("cat sat Daddy" became "the cat sat on top of Daddy," etc.). There was some movement going on, but I could see that Jesse was grinding deeper into his rut of only using "correct" spellings, and so limiting terribly what he might say. He would occasionally snap, when I urged him to perhaps write something *new*, as it was getting a bit boring for me to just read the same thing over and over every day. "But I'm trying to learn all these words *first* before I go on to any others!" Writing was becoming mechanical for him -- he was seeing it as an exercise in penmanship and correct spelling. He still did it willingly and with interest, proud of his growing ease, but I was becoming distressed that he was not seeing writing as a communication tool anymore. I knew, too, that his "plan" to learn each word perfectly before going on to others was a doomed one -- too limiting, too slow. Think how stunted our *oral* vocabularies would be if we had tried that tactic at age two!

Our break-through came when my husband and I both read a book by George Riemer, *How They Murdered the Second "R"*. Among other things, the book strongly advocates using some way of simplifying the sound/spelling correspondences in English for beginning writers, feeling our unreliable language is a terrible trick to play on a little kid. The book is full of wonderful examples of genuine writing done by 6-7 year old children who felt unencumbered by the onus of spelling correctly. These children wrote whatever they could *say*. Their written vocabularies were not limited by what select batch of short vowel words they had just been doled out in reading or spelling class. The book in many ways supports the ideas in

Glenda Bissex's wonderful book, *GNYS AT WRK: A Child Learns to Read and Write*, which describes the author's son's development in writing and reading through his invented spellings. Jesse, unlike Bissex's son Paul, didn't come up with the idea of inventive spelling on his own -- he had apparently never thought of it. To Jesse, spellings were "givens," something you copied and eventually just knew. They come from the outside-in, not the inside out.

Jesse finally understood and took to heart the idea of "sound-spelling" when Howard had Jesse's favorite puppet, Monkey, begin to "sound-spell" messages and questions to Jesse. (Monkey has been a very loved family member for three and a half years now.) Jesse began writing little statements and replies to Monkey, sound-spelling "because Monkey would find it easier to read." The playful situation made it possible for Jesse to not worry about correctness. Howard also wrote out a vowel chart for Jesse (Jesse already knew the sounds of most consonants fairly well), using basically the "Unifon" simplified spelling system (a system where all long vowels are written to this pattern -- *ae, ee, ie, oe, ue,* each sound getting only *one* spelling pattern.) I also was reading Jesse parts of *How They Murdered the Second "R"* aloud, and that also seemed to give him confidence in this new approach. He could readily tell which writings from the book were done by the inventive spellers and which were done by the "Dick and Jane" group -- the latter were stilted and chopped, not at all the natural voices of children.

Within a month, Jesse was writing whole little stories. He was also using written language for real purposes -- little notes to Howard ("Doet feel BADLee DADDY love Jesse I will not teez yoo Tunite"), signs on block buildings or drawings ("Dun Bie Jesse"). In the beginning, writing was incredibly hard work. Jesse would at times burst into frustrated tears when I couldn't make out what he'd written, or sometimes he'd be unable to remember what word it was he was writing as he was so buried in dissecting the smaller sounds within the word. I, too, had a lot of *patience* learning to do. I had to learn not to question or correct his spelling, but just try to do the best I could to understand his *meanings*.

DoeT feeL
BADee DADDy
      LoVe JeSSeT WIL NoT
TeeZ    Yoo TU NITe

    This experience made me realize, again, how valuable parents are as their children's guides and teachers -- just as usually a sensitive parent is the best person to understand a toddler's beginning spoken language, so too, we're the ones most likely to be able to decipher the first rough written words. We know the context of our children's thoughts so well that we're more likely to be able to predict their meanings.

    Jesse needed me to be near physically, while he wrote during his early spurt. He would need to ask me for sounds he didn't know (I was surprised how often *sh*, *th*, *ch*, *ou* -- "harder" sounds we hadn't worked on much before -- came up.). He needed me to reread his writing aloud for him, as at that point he couldn't always read back what he'd written. Letter sounds he'd never been able to remember before now were needed for his writing and he began to forge memory links he'd never had before. I was pleased he would *try* any word at all, long words with several syllables, anything. All words were his.

My mother wondered over Christmas, while delightedly reading Jesse's little note that began "Hie Grammo," when Jesse might ever learn to spell correctly. I've been amazed that the free writing process, coupled with his growing reading, just naturally involves us in discussions about our specific written language and its idiosyncrasies. Through my responding to his questions, Jesse is gaining more and more sense of how our complex code works. As Bissex noted with her son, there is clearly no danger of Jesse developing "bad habits." As his spellings are thought out new each time he meets a word, he is not merely repeating marks on paper that he made once before. Also, Jesse is very aware that he is moving towards "REAL" spelling, and knows that certain situations (addresses on envelopes for instance) are inappropriate places for invented spellings. We've read children's books on the history of our language, and this has helped him understand the somewhat snarled, though rich, roots of English, and so why we have so many odd spellings.

An interesting side benefit of this work is that it's given Jesse a way to observe and learn about some of his articulation difficulties. He usually pronounces "th" as something close to "z," and so in his early writings he'd happily write "zn" for "then." He's now aware of this difference, indeed at times he's *over*-compensated and *over*-generalized, once correcting his "WUZ" ("was") to "WUTH." He also did what John Holt mentioned in an old GWS -- spontaneously wrote "chraen" for "train," and indeed this is closer to what most of us *do* say.

Jesse is no longer so terribly "touchy" about his writing. His handwriting has even improved greatly, and more lower-case letters are proudly sprinkled through his capitals. He needs no reminding about spaces between words, he's gaining rudimentary knowledge of what a sentence is and how we punctuate them (LOVES exclamation points!), and can take low-key questions about sounds he may have left out of a word in mature stride. He writes almost daily, and no longer needs me right with him. He even seems to be enjoying the privacy of writing. We discuss writing a lot, everything from "writer's block" to needs for editing and proofreading for *adult's* writing (he sees *my* rough drafts!), to how writers come up with ideas or how writers borrow and change others ideas, to why most young kids in schools don't write much. (Jesse was astounded to discover our nine year old neighbor clearly felt *copying* an encyclopedia article was "writing"). And Jesse has gone from writing "CAT SAT DADDY" to "Win cats ar siting dan thae git a rool lok" (When cats are sitting down they get a royal look). Why, my wooden sword-loving son even now loves the old saying, "The pen is mightier than the sword." He's thinking like a writer...

### Jacob and Molly Begin Sound-Spelling

One of the nice aspects of getting your first child started with something is that your next children just naturally expect to do the same thing when they get older. So it was with writing. Jacob and Molly just naturally started sound-spelling on their own as soon as they were able.

Here is a caption that Molly (age 4) wrote to a picture that she drew of goldfish swimming in a fishtank (the goldfish are shown looking in the corners for food that was actually floating in the middle of their tank):

> Gold fish swim arownd. They say wars some food!! They swim in the corners!

As Jacob turned four, Susan wrote about Jacob's beginning attempts at writing...

I realize with a certain guilt that Jacob, my second son, has been overlooked somewhat in my writing. We are probably all familiar with the syndrome of taking countless photos of child #1, some mere dozen of child #2, and poor child #3 gets in an occasional holiday shot. (I was a third child myself and know the situation well now from both sides...) So, too, with my writing -- this piece is my rectification. When I told Jacob that I was planning an article about him for the homeschooling newsletter, he got an overwhelming look of gratitude in his

goLD fish Swim arownD.     thɘSbY
      Wors some fooD!! tHey   SWiM
in tHe        Conners!

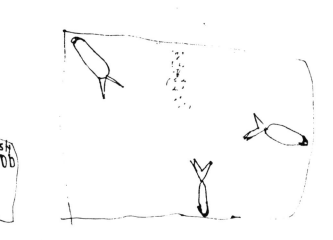

whole body, and said earnestly, "Make it a LONG article, Mommy, very, VERY long!" He understands that to be written about is to be noticed, cherished, regarded as important and worthy of respect. It means that *he* is special, not just a minor character in oblique orbit about a bigger brother.

Jacob feels, now, that it is imperative that *he* show some progress in reading, now that Jesse is moving along with it all. He can usually read his name, he's recognizing more and more alphabet letters, he knows printing carries meaning -- but he's really not ready or wanting to focus on *much* print yet. It's not that he really is asking for help with beginning reading, what is at stake is *keeping up.* Jacob's latest attempt at salvaging his self-esteem has been to proclaim proudly that *he* knows how to read, "that SILENT way" (something he knows Jesse only does occasionally). He will demonstrate his technique for a curious parent or brother -- he gets a knowing look in his eye, posts his finger under the first word in a line chosen at random on a page (he clearly knows our language reads from left to right), slowly moves his finger across the print, and beams widely when he reaches the end. Miracle accomplished -- reading! He knows that no one can challenge him, for he is indeed doing just what he sees the bigger folks doing. The secret is all his. (Reminds me a bit of when Jesse at one and a half used to hum into my recorder before he figured out blowing. He also seemed a bit suspicious that he might be "found out," so he wouldn't keep it up for long... A kazoo at Christmas was the natural solution...)

Jacob's other passionate venture now is writing. He sees Jesse writing daily, sees Jesse receiving personal letters in the mail, and he wants to DO THAT TOO, and so Jacob has his own clipboard, and paper, his own pencils embossed with his name, and he, too, sets out almost daily to write, and his writing is seriously kept in his own specially marked folder and his letters are sent through the mail (his own JACOB RICHMAN address labels affixed to the envelope, on the proper side...). He writes stories, imperiously demanding, "What letter spells 'Today I planted a garden of pumpkin seeds!'" He sprinkles his wobbling letters all about the page, often circling bunches of them to try to show his separate words and sentences. Often he will print batches of letters all over his paper, *without* saying aloud what it is he thinks he's writing, probably without having any idea himself. He then presents the completed writing to me and I must then READ it to him, and I'd better not ask *him* to read it to me, or an overwhelming tantrum will ensue. What is needed is that I say, perhaps, "Oh! I bet this is about little Rabbit Jump-Jump running away from his mother?" (A favorite theme of Jacob's...) If hopefully Jacob answers affirmatively, I can then elaborate, spinning out a whole story on the spot in a definite Reading Voice (Jacob is very sensitive to when people are "just talking"). Howard tries occasionally to feign "silent reading" when perusing these pieces, but Jacob will have none of it, clearly seeing *that* as a hoax on our part -- "READ it!" he insists.

Jacob also knows how Jesse goes about slowly sounding out words he's writing, so he too says his words in slow motion, "*RRRRRRRR -- AAAAAAAA -- BBBB -- IIIII -- TTTTTTTTTTTT* -- what letter makes *TTTTTTTTT*?" He now usually demands, "Is that *all* the letters in *rabbit*?" What *other* letters are there? What other letters are there *that I know*?" Jacob has also discovered writing the "baby" letters. He's been watching my small, scribbly handwriting, and is imitating it, making little squiggling mountains and valleys all across his paper, laid out in neat rows. The feeling of freedom is delicious to him -- this is so fast, so *real* looking, so JUST LIKE WRITING. Interesting, too, that Jacob takes the word "letters" literally -- he "writes letters" to people, which means he writes alphabet letters all about the page, as many as he can squeeze in...

Jacob insists now that I keep writing, more and more -- different from his usual reaction to my writing urges. In fact, he recently dictated in a letter to a little friend that "It is not fun to have a writing Mommy." Guess it all depends on who I'm writing about if he can sense that through my writing, I'm paying more attention to him, not less. I love you, Jacob.

The Picsher Tavern    1\3 0
A86

one year at christmas when we
were in georgia Daddy bought our
first Billy goat To Own. He is gruff
all white though his Beerd is
Stained yellow.

He has no horns they were
Takin of when he was young.
He wasn't born in our barn.
when gruf was first here he was
very shy of people he would
not butt you, like some billy
goats, he would Run in stead,
He is still slightly scared of
people who he does not know.

on the third Sater day in
January Mommy needed to go in
to town. Before that I got all
muddy. the reason was we needed
mor gold fish food,
So I Stayed home Daddy toke a
nap. mommy came home with two
new gold fish and the food of
course

# 7. Becoming a Writer

Many parents have trouble encouraging or helping their children to write on any regular sort of basis. Sometimes they try the same sort of meaningless writing assignments that, with the aid of coercion, get kids to write in school. This method doesn't work well at home. (It doesn't work very well at school either, but that's another story...)

Though most homeschooled kids read up a terrific storm, the majority I know have not had as positive a time with writing. The kids balk at putting pen to paper, the parents try unsuccessfully to "motivate" with cutesy suggestions, then turn to cajoling, then nagging, then it finally all gets dropped. "Maybe he's just not READY to write yet, maybe when he's older..." But when the time does not just come of its own, the parents are left feeling inwardly anxious and guilty, and the kids never get a chance to feel the delight and power of their own writer's voice.

## Writer's Voice

Yet many homeschooled children do write prolifically. They write articles, family newsletters, letters to friends, family books, notes to parents, and for a host of other purposes. The best teachers in schools and homes set up real communications purposes for children to write within. When children are writing to really communicate to someone, writing is not an exercise detached from the real world, but is instead part of the real world.

When children know they are really communicating, listen to the sense of humor and life that their writing sometimes attains. Here are some selections from the

*Rainbow News*, **a family newsletter edited by nine-year Sunny Schaeffer.**

### In the February 1987 issue, Sunny wrote:

Victory! Victory!

It was the first time I had ever played "Risk." Risk is an exciting war game. You win when you've wiped out all the enemy armies, and you become ruler of the world. My 17 year-old brother challenged me to a game. He figured there was no way I could win. He even said he could beat me in 20 turns. (Insult upon insult!) It took 20 turns all right... When the smoke cleared, I was the winner! Mark challenged me to a rematch. It was another 20 turns, and I was still the ruler of the world. Not only was Mark furious, he was totally humiliated. I felt wonderful. I think we should all chip in and buy Reagan and Gorbachev a "Risk" game. They can play at war, and we can get on with our lives!!!!

### Similarly, in the October 1986 issue, Sunny wrote:

Pumping Oatmeal

Well, it's fall, and once again Mark has begun one of his famous "exercise programs." This year Mark set a new record for himself, he pulled a muscle after 4 weeks and has been sitting on the bench ever since. Come on, Mark! When are you going to get off the bench?

### In the November 1986 issue, Mark replied:

Misinformed

To Whom it may concern:
To say I was outraged when I read the article "Pumping Oatmeal" is an understatement. I am very surprised that such a reputable newspaper would publish these falsehoods. It is true I started a weight training program. After four weeks I pulled a muscle and was sidelined, but I am now back on schedule. I feel the editor of this paper would fear for her physical safety considering I can lift her in the air with my little finger. I trust your paper will stick to the facts in the future.

**Putting out a Newspaper**
Like several other homeschooling children, Jesse
sometimes puts out his own newspaper.

The *Picksher Tavern* began last winter.  It is my eight year
old son Jesse's imaginary newspaper, begun on his own, totally
his own idea.  It is imaginary, partly because the "news" is
largely imagined news, the charge for it sometimes imagined
money, but yet the little paper has become quite a reality for all
of us.

I don't think any of us remember now just how the idea for
the Picksher Tavern evolved.  It came on a backdrop of our
reading *Johnny Tremain* with its colorful world of Revolutionary
War newspapers.  Also we'd read a few other articles and books
about the history of newspapers in England and America.  And
then, as Howard noted, it really wasn't so strange perhaps that
Jesse came up with a newspaper idea, as we're so involved as a
family in putting out the Western PA Homeschoolers Newsletter.
Newsletter talk is always going on around here.

We'd also had a long spell where Jesse had done very little
writing, and we were slowly getting back to a rhythm of daily
writing.  It was almost painfully slow, and Jesse had real trouble
finding a writing theme that he could really sink his teeth into,
feel involved with, feel his writer's voice.  The Picksher Tavern
became his vehicle.

Seems to me Jesse began work on his first issue (or "ishoo,"
as he spelled it) while I was busy with bed-making or laundry
sorting.  He suddenly popped in on me with the announcement
that a newspaper was ready for delivery.  He was both editor and
newsboy, talking in their proper voices and attitudes.    I
responded as a proper customer, not as a teacher with red pencil
in hand, and looked over the little paper with delight.  Jesse had
never come up with such an idea before.

The first issues came out every few days, and had regular
"features" -- a farm comic strip (usually about troubles with goat
milking and cats and mice), a simple maze, a car and truck race
game (similar to one in a math book of his).  The paper had no

real "articles" at that point, no extended writing. Jesse made himself an "office," wrote a sign saying "Pikshr Tavern" to go above the doorway, and was in business. Jacob, Molly, Howard and I were his best (if only) customers. This was all work that Jesse went to readily and eagerly -- it was, after all, totally his own and was to him a wonderful and elaborate play idea.

After a few weeks though, the idea seemed to reach a natural saturation point, a boredom point when it was becoming repetitive and somewhat pointless. Nothing was moving in the idea, and so Jesse moved on to other writing. He became quite involved with keeping a journal, after we'd seen and read the Jeffrey kids' home-bound books. The newspaper was left and forgotten, stored in a file.

But it was not lost. I'm becoming more and more aware of this special value in our homeschooling -- ideas are never really totally dropped. They may hibernate for a while, even a long while, but they can be readily picked up later. I don't think this sort of spiral movement, circling back to bring something old into a new present, can happen readily in schools. If Jesse had begun the Picksher Tavern in a school (highly unlikely anyhow), then dropped the idea, and picked it up later with another teacher, the new teacher could have no sense of the continuity involved. At home the "teacher" doesn't change, so I could see and appreciate what was happening.

Jesse came back to the Picksher Tavern months later, at the beginning of summer. Perhaps it was important that he'd had another short time of little writing. Perhaps the comfort and ready format of the Picksher Tavern gave him a needed starting place, an easy beginning. He greeted his old issues with a touching fondness, almost with the excitement he feels when one of our long gone wild in the woods cats returns for a few days. He remembered just how he'd had his "office," made a new sign, and delved right in. This time, the large amount of writing he'd done over the spring really showed. He now had bonafide lead articles, with a stronger voice, often imitating newspaper style:

U.S. officials say America is making too much stuff and is

> wasting too much and it should not keep garbage rates down.
> For example [spelled "for idzmpl"] Spain or even better
> France makes much less than us. Their garbage cans are 1
> foot when U.S. has 3 feet.

There were also now lots of ads for "gerog sales and okshins," a part of newspapers he gathered seemed to be important to me perhaps! He readily compared his new issues with his old, and was proud of his clearly evident growth -- "In my first issues there was really hardly any writing, now there's a LOT... My mazes in the first issues were so simple, now I'm making much more complicated ones."

He also evolved a whole imagined scenario to explain why the paper had not been published for a good while:

> Talk from Picksher Tavern. We have been having trouble
> since the press broke shortly after Christmas and we had a
> strike also. Most of the workers got new jobs and we had to
> train new workers.

A competitor newspaper came on the scene, the Depot News, which tried to steal business from the Picksher Tavern, and there was some rather cut-throat journalism going on between the two rivals. Again, Jesse would set to this work with no prompting, often writing up a page or more before breakfast.

We set off on a family trip at the end of June, and the Picksher Tavern and Depot News came too. Jesse brought his markers, clipboards and lots of paper, and literally spent hours during our long car rides busily writing and drawing for his papers. He developed a delightful type of person drawing, patterned with intricate symmetrical designs, and he added one of these to the back page of each issue. (Incidentally, the timing of this renewed interest was good for ME, as one stop on our trip was the Mid-Atlantic Homeschooling Conference organized by Manfred Smith, where I was to co-lead a discussion on encouraging children's writing.)

Back from our three week trip, the Picksher Tavern got another boost. We'd bought 2 gelatin hectograph print sets from our local office supply store, on sale for a dollar each, and Jesse was eager to try actually making printed copies of his paper.

This real publishing effort gave Jesse the motivation to polish up his pieces a bit -- he now wrote first drafts, asked for and accepted a bit of spelling help, tried hard to write neatly (always a struggle for him -- he has typical "boys" handwriting). He wrangled with the sometimes cantankerous technology of the simple presses, and asked lots of questions about other types of printing methods. He'd had a chance to try out a Ben Franklin press at the Capitol Children's Museum in Washington, D.C., and we often visit local print shops for a quick look at the astonishing clanking machines and to pick up any extra scrap paper the shops don't want. We also read a short biography of Guttenburg in here somewhere.

After a bit the Picksher Tavern was laid aside again, becoming once more a bit stale. Jesse turned, refreshed, to other writing -- longer 200 word pieces telling about his new goldfish, our monarch butterfly hatchings, his new stone buildings dotting the woods and yards. We began a helpful way of rewriting and editing, an idea I got from Madalene Murphy in her work with her son Christian. I'd take Jesse's first draft, type it out on our computer/printer exactly as he'd written it, same invented spellings, lack of capitalization, lack of punctuation. I'd print out a copy with big print, and quadruple spacing -- plenty of room for Jesse to make corrections and changes. It seemed much easier for him to make changes on these print-outs, as there was not the aesthetic trauma of marking up and possibly ripping his own paper. He'd sometimes go through and change all the small *i*'s to capital *I*'s, or go through and add in punctuation marks, or find all the words that rhymed with "all" that he'd spelled "ol." I might ask him to try to find, say, ten words that he thought might be misspelled, and see if he could figure out closer spellings. He often could. If he knew a word was not quite right, but didn't know what to do with it, I'd underline the letters he'd gotten RIGHT, saying maybe, "Hmm, 4 out of 6 letters are correct, one needs to be deleted, and one exchanged for another." Figuring out correct spellings became a sort of game, a type of code cracking. Almost fun.

### EDITING A ROUGH DRAFT

Susan typed the rough draft just as Jesse had written it with paper and pencil.  Then Jesse edited the typed copy. The final copy, which went into The Animals of Richman Farm appears at the bottom.

Orange Juice is good yoomerd and lite orange, He. is

a prity good mouse kachr, But he is Quite scard of

his twin berother Timithee. Orange Juice is a

                      neighbors
wanderer he gos to the ~~naibrs~~ and raids the garbigا

          so duse his foTher mer,
cans: he is very kind to the kitins hoo he is the

fother and the brothr to.

ORANGE JUICE
      by Jesse Richman

Orange Juice is good humored and light orange.  He
is a pretty good mouse catcher, but he is quite
scared of his twin brother, Timothy.  Orange Juice
is a wanderer.  He goes to the neighbors and raids
the garbage cans.  So does his father Mer.  He is
very kind to the kittens, who he is the brother to.

Jesse has now used some of these computer printed out stories as lead articles for the Picksher Tavern. He's even talking about using a simple block-printing method to add on his masthead at the top. Using the computer has not turned Jesse away from handwriting though -- he last week put out another hectographed copy, and even then copied out his lead article once again by hand, as he wasn't quite satisfied with the clarity of the printing. His head is full of ideas to extend the paper, and I'm sure it will keep popping up from time to time over the next couple of years. The Picksher Tavern has become a sort of measuring stick to see how his writing is growing and changing, as well as an old and welcome friend. It will be almost sad if he ever starts spelling it "PICTURE Tavern!"

## Making Books

Some families may have heard of the idea of making their own books with their kids. I'd like to take you through some book-making projects we've done, just to show some of the process that can be involved. And lest you begin thinking that elaborate bookbinding is not for you, remember that "publishing" can be very simple. Roy Clark says in *Free to Write* that parents are actually publishing when they pin a child's story up on the humble refrigerator door. The important thought in publishing should be using it as a chance to recognize a child's work and give the child a real audience.

But on to some specifics, some things that have been tried in families.

One of our first forays into bookmaking was making our own blank books that the kids could then write in (making your own version of the lovely cloth bound "anything books" you can buy in book stores...). We were first inspired in this just after visiting with another family whose kids wrote in homemade books regularly. We were caught by the idea, and the next day we were folding and sewing signatures, cutting cardboard for making "hardbacks," choosing calico fabric for the covers, figuring out how to glue in end pages without getting them rippled and gloppy -- and when we were all done, the boys were awed.

REAL BOOKS. They turned the books over and over in their hands lovingly, saying over and over how they were just like REAL BOOKS. They were so clearly a cut above the simple stapled together affairs we'd made before, that they inspired a new burst of writing activity. Jesse used his as a daily journal for a year, and having all his writing in this one place gave a graphic showing of both how his ideas grew over time, and also how his handwriting gradually improved. He went from writing two sentence entries to long, several paragraph descriptions. Two years later Jesse still loves rereading his journal -- amazed at his earlier inventive spellings, enjoying remembering long forgotten incidents (like the time Jacob had cried after losing a tiny toy, his loved "cow mechanic," somewhere on the way to the barn, and how he, Jesse, had tried to find something else to replace it for him, and then how I was able to find the toy in the grass...).

Another way we've approached book-making is by gradually realizing that we have some writing that we want to share with others. Maybe a certain event is coming up where we want to present our ideas, and so a book project becomes a natural extension of our other studies. Our first work in this way was our Monarch Butterfly Book. For this our binding was "pre-fab" -- when we'd typed up our stories about caterpillar raising and butterfly hatchings and departings, we simply bought a magnetic page photo album and laid everything out, along with photos and drawings of our experiences. The result was pleasing and complete and very finished looking, and gave the whole project much more of a sense of closure than just having our stories scattered in folders getting dog-eared. We felt published. We shared this book at a Homeschooler's Science Fair, lent it out to several families. We enjoyed looking through it again ourselves this past summer when monarch caterpillars were once more eating milkweed leaves in jars in our project room, and we were once more watching them change to chrysalises and emerge with damp wings. It was special to have our OWN book to read as a reference this time, not just the "official" books other folks had written about the subject.  We were also authors whose words could be kept over time.

Our next book making project grew out of a visit to another homeschooling family.  The boy, Brian Coughenour, showed me a journal he had just begun two days before, telling about the animals he owns at his small farm.  He was a child who previously had NO interest in writing, who thought he didn't need to write because he could already form his letters, and he DID write his MATH problems out anyway.

His mother in despair called a friend for advice.  That mother had the wonderful good sense to put her own 8 year old on the phone to tell Brian about HIS chicken journal he'd just started, detailing the goings on of his very loved chickens.  Brian was hooked, ended the phone conversation giving his friend a suggestion on what he might add next about the chickens, and said he thought he'd better go to begin his own story of his goat!

I'd read Brian's two entries aloud to Jesse and Jacob and they enjoyed them, and we talked about the idea of an animal journal on the car ride home.  I then thought of the delightful book, *Our Animal Friends at Maple Hill Farm* by Alice and Martin Provenson, which the boys both love, and wondered aloud if maybe we could write a similar book about the animals of RICHMAN FARM.  We were ALL hooked.  The theme was a good one for us, as we first of all found that we already had some material for the book -- Jesse had always loved to write about the goats and cats and goldfish and sheep, and had quite a few promising rough drafts lying about.  I wrote mostly about the animals that had died when the kids were very young, or even before they were born, keeping alive the stories that might have gradually faded away, forgotten.  It was vital here that I was a contributing writer also -- I was not just a "director," but a participant, and so, eligible to have my fair say over how the whole work was moving along, and ready to share my writing triumphs and troubles with the kids.  Jacob dictated his stories, and even Howard added one story once he'd seen our completed rough copy.  We all worked at illustrations, using line drawings and simple block printing techniques.

The project naturally brought out discussion of the parts a book needed -- title page, table of contents, dedication. We worked on lay out together, had our rough mock-up xeroxed, and were ready to begin the actual bookbinding. Jesse designed a print for the fabric cover, we collated the pages, brainstormed over the best way to bind it together (couldn't sew signatures this time as we didn't have double pages to work with) and somehow actually got it all finished by Christmas. Again, the kids were amazed at how "real" these books looked. And now we'd even made multiple COPIES of a book, and the kids pretended we had our own bookstore. (Complete stock consisting of 8 hardbacks, and 12 paperbacks -- we'd learned how time consuming binding the hardbacks was -- this is no project for the rushed or harried or over-extended among us!)

As a final culmination I sent a copy of *The Animals of Richman Farm* on to the Provensens, along with a cover letter letting them know how they had inspired our work. How special to get back a personal and encouraging reply, another link to the real world of authors and books. But perhaps the very best result of making the book was having the chance to later read the long family book written by our homeschooling friends, the Wilcoxes, telling about their two month trip to Mexico. We had inspired someone else now!

We'd slacked off bookbinding for a while when another homeschooling family, the Stockwells, invited us to participate in a small bookbinding class they were offering at their home. Tricia organized the day very well. She shared with the kids the many different ways that books can be put together, and had a whole pile of books for them to sort by type of binding. She read the delightful book by Aliki telling about the long process an author/illustrator goes through to take a book from vague idea to completed product ready to be marketed. Then the kids had a chance to make their own simple books, using vinyl wallpaper samples as the soft cover. This made a quite attractive and long-lasting cover, and is certainly easier to do than trying for hardbacks. With sewn signatures the books had a much better look and feel than a stapled together job. After this, we got hooked on making simple wallpaper cover books whenever we needed new notebooks for something-- we could whip one up in less than a half-hour (a good project for the short-of-time home binder!)

We learned about another type of simple bookmaking from Fullis Conroy. She has made each of her kids several well-loved books by using small pieces of brightly colored poster board as pages, punching two holes in the edges, and joining them all together with ring binders. One nice advantage of this type of book is that you can add to the book at any time -- just open the ring and slip in another card. Fullis covers each page with clear contact, making these books ideal for the littlest homeschoolers. They've made alphabet books, simple story books, books for each child, and even a terrific photo book with captions all about all the types of trucks and vehicles and road graders and bulldozers and backhoes that her 2 year old son Silas loves.

The boys recently went through another good cycle of book writing, but when we were ready for publishing and binding I have to admit I inwardly groaned. I was tired, I was busy, I didn't have the time for all the cutting and gluing and measuring. BUT we were about to go on a long family trip and wanted to bring the kids' books along as gifts, so we knew we had to do something. Our local quick copy center came to our rescue -- after making us up a number of copies of Jesse's book, they suggested we might want them to put a plastic comb binding on it. How simple! How cheap! The kids got to see the little machine that punched all the little rectangular holes and inserted the binding. This did just the right trick of helping the book feel official and finished. And when Jacob saw Jesse's spiral bound book, he immediately got to work finishing his poem book that he'd been lagging on, and we even had his ready for Grandma.

And of course don't forget the easiest bookbinding technique -- stapling together the separate sheets of paper with a simple cover. Even this little bit of care can turn the simplest story into something special, worthy of special handling and a special place on your bookshelf.

### Rough Drafts
**Writing does not begin in final form. When Jesse was eight, Susan wrote about the process of working through rough drafts in her own writing and with Jesse in his writing...**

I've been noticing a lot lately how many simple errors I make in my rough draft writing, and it's helping me to be more tolerant of my 8 year old son Jesse's rough drafts. I'm learning to give him the same time and consideration I give myself with my writing. I don't expect my writing to be ready for publishing on the first go round, and I no longer expect his to look that way either.

I recently looked over some of my hastily penciled out paragraphs and found these "errors" -- I'd written *my* for *me*, *ant* for *was*, *of* for *from*, *their* for *they're*, *like* instead of *lick*, and *what* for *who*. I've left out connecting words, and gone back over to rather messily insert them. I've scratched out lots of words and squeezed in substitutes above them that most people probably can't decipher. I've scribbled out whole sentences, XXXX'd out whole paragraphs, put arrows winging across a page to show a possible rearrangement. I've written too small. I've written sideways up a margin. I've written long words with a mere jiggle or scrawl for the last 7 letters. (After all, I know what it means, so what does it matter -- at another stage I can type it all out, letter by letter.)

The "chef d'oeuvre" of my recently noticed rough draft mistakes was a real surprise. I was typing out a copy of a short piece I'd written for a book the kids and I recently put together called *The Animals of Richman Farm*. My story was about the ladybug hibernation spot we'd discovered in a pasture. I had to look twice -- no, surely it couldn't be -- had I really written not once but TWO TIMES -- *labybug*, substituting a *b* for a *d*?!? I couldn't believe it. Now, I have no "directional difficulties," no "dyslexia," no "perceptual problems," and I've known my right from my left since I was five. What my error meant was just that this paper WAS a rough draft, and my thoughts had been racing fast (with maybe a tumbling baby on my lap to boot...). That's all. I didn't need to do workbook exercises or drills to correct my "disability" in recognizing or forming a *b* or *d*. I just needed to do a second draft of my piece.

Now, Jesse LOVED hearing about my *labybug* incident, as he has been known to spell his brother's name as *Jacod* more than once or twice. I try now to let Jesse see my rough drafts, and see what adult writers go through in the writing process. It's really helped him view HIS writing as a series of drafts, and not just as a one shot deal that must be perfect the first time or else. He has plenty of time to reread his pieces for clarity, for spelling, for cohesion. For some kids, writing must seem to be some magic procedure -- POOF! and ideas spring forth onto the page fully proper and correct and ready for an audience. There's no hint of the scratch outs, the corrections, the redrafts, the scissors-and-tape, and most importantly the continual rethinking that goes into most writing.

### Editing on the Computer

When I was an undergraduate student at Carnegie-Mellon University, I used to wonder about the students who spent day and night at the computer center. My friends and I used to call them the computer "nerds" because they had no interest in anything but computers. I got a small glimpse, myself, of the attraction of computers when I took a single course in the FORTRAN computer language, enough to see that it could be fun to play with a computer. In those days all contact with computers was through cards punched on a card-punching machine and the computer's reply spewed out on a rapid-fire printer. The cards would be fed into the computer and thirty minutes later the printer would spew forth explaining why it would not accept your cards. This process would continue from about 10 PM until about 4 AM at which point your exhaustion would disappear in the ensuing feeling of triumph.

That was 1971. I didn't have any more contact with computers until 1983. I wasn't yet a computer "nerd," but I was partly hooked. In 1983 the school I worked for got its first micro-computer. As soon as it arrived, I got a workbook for the BASIC computer language and a manual for the computer's word processing program, and I was soon staying late after school designing educational computer programs to use with my students and typing term papers. I can now proudly claim to be a self-made "nerd."

Some people have mis-supposed that since I am so interested in computers, maybe my children are doing wonderful things on our computers at home. Maybe they are getting prepared for twenty-first century careers as computer whizzes. Actually, my children have really not shown much interest in programming. Sure, they hear my agony as my microcomputer tells me that there is an error in my current program, and sure they hear my exuberation when I get my program to work, but they are not naturally "nerds" and don't seem to show any inclination to be.

Susan is very practical in her use of the computer. With great reluctance she began to do her typing on the computer and soon found it to be a great tool. As she points out, her ten typos per line no longer show up in her final copy. Although she showed no initial enthusiasm as I computerized our newsletter's directory and mailing labels, she did come to appreciate the time-saving result.

Jesse has generally taken on Susan's attitude. I have had more hope for Jacob and Molly. Jacob likes to draw pictures and play games on the computer. Molly mostly uses our electric typewriter which she calls her computer. (Now that we do our typing on the computer, the electric typewriter doesn't get much other use.)

About a year ago, Susan began using the computer to get Jesse to edit his own writing. She would type Jesse's rough drafts onto the computer just as he had written them out with paper and pencil. Then she would print out the drafts and Jesse would mark his changes on the print-out. She would then type Jesse's corrections and print out a revised draft. Still, Jesse wasn't actually doing any of the computer work himself.

For the last couple of days though, Jesse has begun to make changes in his own rough drafts on the computer. A few mornings ago, I showed him a command in WordStar, our word-processing program, that would allow him to correct a particular misspelling everywhere that it occurred in his essay. Incidentally, a "word processing program" is something you buy that makes it easy for you to type whatever you want on your computer. It allows you to type, change, and otherwise manipulate the words in your document. Jesse was writing a story about one of our mother cats named "Moppit." He had frequently misspelled "mopet" and with this command he was able to correct them all at once. He was surprised to find that Susan didn't know that particular WordStar command. I explained that Susan had never worked her way through the WordStar manual and that there were a lot of WordStar commands that she didn't know.

That evening I asked Jesse if he wanted to work his way through the manual and he said he did, so I helped him get set up with the manual in a cookbook holder next to the computer. Then I sat in a nearby chair so that I was available to answer any questions that he asked, and to be an audience if he wanted to show off something that he had just learned. Several times he called me over to show me WordStar commands that he had just learned about. Some of them were new to me. Jesse worked through several pages in the manual, and experimented with several different commands, learning through trial and error.

I don't think Jesse is about to become a computer "nerd," but I do think that computers will be a tool that he is able to use. For a couple of years now, Susan and I have been doing our writing in front of a computer video screen, and now

Jesse is joining us in that adult world.

## Write From The Start

I began this chapter by noting that the artificial-assignment writing model that is common in the schools often does not work at home. It usually does not work well in the schools either. The best writing teachers have argued for years that these sort of assignments do not develop a love for writing in the student. Recently, Susan reviewed *Write From the Start* by Donald Graves and Virginia Stuart[2] which advocates a different approach to writing in the schools and at home...

It seems, in informally talking with many parents, that although most homeschooled kids become eager readers, writing seems to be a bit sluggish for many, a chore, certainly no delight. I hope this book will help all of you gain more pleasure from your writing. I think you'll gain insight into the writing process, you'll be inspired to look at the writing model you present to your kids, you'll become ready to observe a PROCESS rather than dictate it's every step. You'll probably even become more of a writer yourself, if the book has it's proper impact.

A word about the title of the book. It means kids can write, right from the start, at whatever point they are at. We don't have to wait until they are perfect spellers, understand all punctuation and capitalization rules, know about paragraphing format, or know nouns from verbs. They don't even need to know all of the alphabet letters, or both upper and lower case. Kids can begin writing NOW -- but they can't begin writing RIGHT, right from the start. Too many children, teachers, and probably parents, feel kids can't write because their writing is incorrectly spelled, is too slow, too wrong in every way. They are criticized immediately to a jolting silent halt.

---

[2]Available from your bookstore, or from E. P. Dutton Publishers, 2 Park Avenue, New York, NY 10016, for $16.95 hardback. Or ask your library to order it.

A thing I like about this book is that it's clearly directed to parents as well as teachers in schools, and the descriptions of good school writing programs can easily be mentally translated into homeschooling.   Homeschooling is not specifically mentioned, but when I wrote to Donald Graves to tell him how much I'd enjoyed the book, and how useful I felt it could be to homeschoolers, I found he was very interested in hearing about homeschooler's experiences with writing.   He wrote that he'd met John Holt a year and a half ago at a conference in Nova Scotia, and that John had been very interested then in hearing about his work.   I think they have a lot in common philosophically. Graves has a similar trust in kids. For example, he urges us to trust kids to be able to come up with ideas for writing THEMSELVES.   Our role is not to rack our brains thinking up clever and cute story-starters and motivations and "tricks" but rather to be colleagues for our children, respect their efforts, help them talk about the writing process, and show them what the usually hidden writing process can be like.   In John Holt's phrase, give kids access to the world of writing.

In a chapter called "Wrong from the Start," the book has a great expose of writing as it is usually taught in schools.  Could be very handy to you in trying to clarify to your school district what your approach to writing is -- and therefore why you may not want to use their English textbooks.  Graves blasts the "skill and drill" component approach that tears all whole activities down into minute digestible bits, losing all flavor of the original activity.  He feels that kids spend all their time in most schools PREPARING to write -- doing fill-in-the-blank exercises about vocabulary, circling the correct multiple choice answer about punctuation, or merely copying a sentence or two from the blackboard or workbook.  If the students do actually write something, it is immediately judged, marked up with red pencil, graded -- then tossed out.  The child is not given the time and support to work through several drafts himself, to find his real writers' voice, to find what it is he really wants to say.  He is not given a real audience for his work, a real purpose.   Just assignments, just bits and pieces. Just "getting ready."

In contrast, Graves and Stuart offer concrete vignettes of many children of all ages, at home and at school, who are feeling like writers and who are writing a lot, almost every day. I think these parts of the book would be great to read aloud to our kids (mine loved it). It could help kids see how other kids' writing can change and grow over time. My feeling is that many kids who balk at writing, who writhe and squirm away from it, who seem to insist on being perfectionists (therefore they can't and won't try), may just have no sense of the process ALL writers go through. They don't yet write themselves, and they see only the finished, magically perfect, printed-up versions of other people's writing. Hearing the stories of the real children in this book could open up a new world for them, a new set of possibilities.

This book has really made a lot of difference in our writing at home. It has helped me see better the ways in which I can support Jesse and Jacob and Molly as beginning writers. How to listen better to their ideas of how their writing is progressing, how to be a better sounding board as Jesse tosses around possible ideas for stories. How to not over-react to details (spelling, punctuation, neatness, etc.) when he's only on the first draft. Often now I ask Jesse to read aloud to me from his drafts, while I sit across the room, so that I can respond first to the sense and meaning of his piece -- I can't react with a critical eye to spelling errors that I can't see. Jesse often picks up small errors himself when he reads aloud to me like this -- sees where he's left out a word, or written the wrong word by mistake. I also discuss my own writing with the kids more, often writing at the same time with them, sometimes on a joint project. In our "Animals of Richman Farm" book we all wrote sections, all of us contributing our own voices and memories to make a larger whole, better than anything we could have done separately.

Another emphasis in the book at first eluded me, as far as translating the idea into homeschooling terms. Graves and Stuart put a lot of emphasis on sharing writing with others, telling of lively classrooms where children can borrow hardbound copies of books written by classmates.  Then it hit -- why not share more writing among homeschooled children?  The BACKPACK certainly does this, but even more, we are now trying to send more writing through the mail to specific friends.  After all, as Jesse said today, that's what the mail is for, sharing writing. And whenever we visit a family these days, seems a child is always bringing me some writing to look over, and it's always a delight, and something I always call my kids over to see.  Brian Coughenour showed me his new animal journal, John Stephen Fredland showed us the very long sports adventure book he's been working on for several months, and the Kissell girls showed us their handbound journals.

We're beginning to get writing in the mail too -- a wonderful book by Willy Moffatt about a lonely fir tree wishing he were a Christmas tree, and a whole series of memories of his summer trips by Luke Wilson.  Takes a bit of time of course, a bit of effort to xerox our kids writing, or write out extra copies, or bind a small book, but the rewards are coming in and making it all worthwhile.  I also think it can help kids (and parents!) to physically see another kids' rough drafts -- to see that others may not print neatly either, or spell expertly, or whatever, but what good stories they may have to tell!

Another thing that Graves and Stuart point to again and again is that teachers and parents who want their kids to write need to write themselves, they need to go through the process, often time-consuming and difficult, of trying to get their own thoughts on paper.  There's lots here to encourage the adults who have felt for years that writing is not for them, that they just can't do it. The teachers in Graves' study often began finding their writer's voice when they began keeping journals and personal written observations about individual children who were in their classes. Likewise, I think many of us parents are finding our true writer's voice when we begin writing about our own children.  I always think that when we write about our children it's like a special gift for them -- we're letting them know that they are important enough for us to take the time to keep our memories about them in writing. And our newsletter, *Pennsylvania Homeschoolers* gives us all a place to share with others, others who are not critical but who will love hearing your stories.

**Other Good Books on Writing**
There are many other fine books coming out now about writing with children, in fact almost an overwhelming number. One possible criteria to use when you try to decide which to borrow or buy -- flip through the book to see if there are any examples of actual children's writing included along with the text. If there are, I'll wager it's a decent book that you and your kids can really gain from. I always read my three the actual samples of kids writing that I find in these books and they always want me to read more and more, and soon I can see how these concrete examples have become little inspirations to them. And often, the kids even want me to read what the adult author said about a certain child's piece, and we discuss together our own reactions.

In *Responding to Children's Writing*[3] Susannah Sheffer, editor of *Growing Without Schooling*, talks about the early stages of scribble writing, moving into invented spellings, finding different real audiences for writing, revising writing in response to a reader's questions or comments, and helping children learn about, and perhaps work with, adult writers. Susannah also gives suggestions for helping kids get together regularly for writer's workshops so that they can share their writing regularly with one another. The booklet is an excellent introduction to thinking about our role with our kids' writing as more than just eyeballing spelling errors or punctuation mistakes. It is full of stories of actual children and parents that Susannah has worked with over the years. My son Jesse, now 10, has participated in several writers' workshops that Susannah has led and has always come out happy and energized -- and writing! This booklet is

---

[3]Available from John Holt's Book and Music Store, Holt Associates, 2269 Massachusetts Ave., Cambridge MA 02140, 14 pages, $3.00, phone: 617–864–3100.

like having Susannah talking with you, sharing her good love of writing and inspiring us all on.

*Free to Write,*[4] by Roy Peter Clark, advocates opening up to young writers the ways of working that the best journalists use, feeling that journalism indeed holds a key to honing kids' writing skills.  He talks about the whole writing process -- brainstorming to get ideas, researching, interviewing, notetaking, rough drafts (this chapter is appropriately called "Making A Mess" and even has some astonishing photocopies of adult writers' VERY messy first drafts), editing, writing every day, publishing stories (and he sees that even posting a story on the humble refrigerator door is a simple form of publishing...), evaluation, writing anxiety, and more.

One of the best sections of the book is "Celebrate Student Writing," which includes the best writing of dozens of children the author met and worked with in St. Petersburg, Florida.  I think our homeschooled kids benefit immensely from hearing high quality writing done by students -- their expectations for their own writings rise, they come to realize that they too might write something that gripping or humorous or evocative.  Clark also shows us HOW these fine pieces moved through many stages to get to their polished, published form.

The book is practical, concrete, a delight to read, inspiring from first to last.  You'll come out of this book a better writer yourself, too, more aware of what good writers are doing with their craft.

I could go on and on about these books and the good ideas in them.  I hope that you find them, or books like them, and get inspired.  And anytime you or your kids have some writing to share -- feel very welcome to send it on!

---

[4]Available from Heinemann Educational Books, Inc., 70 Court St, Portsmouth, NH 03801, 281 pages, $15.00.

# 8. Math

Schools generally teach math in cookbook fashion. Often, the children are learning to use recipes without understanding why the recipe works, or even what the recipe is trying to accomplish. In this chapter, Susan shares some of the ways we have approached math in our home, starting with Jesse as a young child of four learning about measurement and shapes.

## Measurement and Shapes

Two nights ago, I told Jesse (4) the funny story I'd read a few years back about a king who measured a proposed bed using *his* feet, only to have the much smaller carpenter make it by measuring with his own *smaller* feet -- a story about the need for a standard unit of measure. We cut ourselves wooden rulers (free scrap wood, of course) that were as long as our *own* feet, six for each of us and we began exploring measurements around the house -- how many of Jesse's rulers would fit across his toy store? His chair's legs? Our piano bench? His bulldozer shovel? Jesse set to work eagerly, seeing just what had to be done.

We right away faced the problem of needing divisions of our rulers -- often a little bit of the last ruler would hang out over the edge. I suggested we might draw marking lines on our rulers, to show where the objects actually ended. A marker was brought out, the lines drawn. At first I thought I'd need to urge him to mark out even "units" -- halves, thirds, etc. I soon realized that Jesse himself could sense the need for more markings, and the more concretely that need was felt, the better. Always we compared one length to another, making guesses and estimates --

"I wonder if the piano bench is as long as the tunnel? Is Daddy's briefcase as long as the chess board?" -- I was struck by the very intelligent common sense approach Jesse used in all this. He'd put series of new markings as needed, always being delighted and amazed when one of his "old" lines helped to pinpoint a new length. His estimates and comparisons were always quite accurate. And how easy it will be for him, when he eventually goes to use "real" rulers, to understand *why* there are all those little lines all over them. And *I'll* always remember the spirit of discovery, the creative thinking, the excitement and energy of that evening. How refreshingly different from a textbook approach to measuring!

Another fun toy that allows a child to assimilate quite a lot of mathematical thinking gradually is the geo-board. We've made a variety of sizes, depending on what size wood we've scrounged. The making is simple -- find a square piece of plywood or particle board, measure off an array of points to form a grid, hammer in 1" finishing nails, get a pack of assorted rubber bands, and start experimenting with shapes, lines, and designs. My son began using one when he was two years old -- at first the challenge was simply to get a rubber band stretched from nail to nail without it popping back at him. Soon he discovered opening a line into a triangle or square. Now at 4 1/2 he experiments with triangles inside of triangles, makes symmetrical patterns, rectangles, diamonds, and an occasional hexagon. This play has also made my son spot stray rubber bands wherever he goes: "Put this in your pocket, Mommy -- we could use it with my geo-boards."

Also, lately we've gathered up quite a collection of small ceramic tiles -- the type used on bathroom floors. We found sheets of "sample" tiles discarded behind a flooring store. We pried the little squares, rectangles, and large squares off their backing boards, and now have a wonderful new building toy. As Jesse makes pretend boats and buildings, he also muses aloud about how two small squares make a rectangle, and two rectangles make a big square, etc. We've retrieved half a floor's worth of 1" square tiles from a demolished house. (A bit of washing, and some hammer blows to loosen the cement on the edges, and they look quite respectable!) And most recently we made a real find -- a set of 4-inch hexagonal tiles, again tossed out by a store. Our eyes are really becoming trained -- we're suddenly noticing all loosened tiles everywhere. Who says mathematics isn't part of the real world?

## Math and Money

Jesse (5), a budding consumer at garage sales and food co-ops, is beginning to really want to understand money values. What will this bunch of coins in his pocket buy at the hardware store? What is this business of pennies, nickels, dimes, quarters, and dollar bills? What's the sense of it? He's understanding clearly now that it's a good trick to only carry ONE dime rather than TEN pennies -- saves all that counting out and doesn't take up so much room in a pocket, a good invention. We've read a children's book on the history of money and he was quite intrigued. Could see that coins were a bit handier to tote about than goats or sheep for barter.

Then one day, as we were meandering through the Pittsburgh Carnegie Museum, we stumbled upon a small exhibit of old money. I boosted him up to see the odd bills with strange faces on them, the old lumpy coins, different sizes than ours. Talked a bit again about how money was an invention, something that's changed with time as people get new ideas, or as new governments take over. Then Jesse pointed out what seemed to be some broken or cut coins. We read the accompanying card and discovered we were looking at the original U.S. quarter! A silver dollar CUT into 4 bits! The pieces were shaped just like the "quarters" Jesse knew from our Sunday morning waffles. What a good laugh we had over this all. And Jesse on his own said that probably after a while they just decided to make quarters a separate round shape so that people would stop cutting up all the dollars. So Jesse now has a real visualization of what "four quarters equals one dollar" really means -- it's quite literally just like our four sections of waffle making one big round one.   And they actually used to cut them up!   What serendipity is possible with this homeschooling, the possibilities of coming upon these gems that help everything fall into place in new ways!

Now contrast this incident with this picture of a "wonderful" kindergarten that a friend enthusiastically described to me right around the same time as this museum visit, and you might get a clearer picture of how our learning at home is unique and so special.  The kindergarten teacher, it seemed, had just completed a unit on "Money" with the class.  I'm sure they did their share of xerox sheets on matching coin values, maybe used plastic coins or maybe dollar bill stamp pads.  The grand culmination of the "unit" was that the teacher actually *took the class down to the supermarket, and they each got to buy a doughnut for a dime!* I'm sure it was a "cute" field trip, with the children probably walking along the road in double file holding hands, looking a bit awed at being out of the building and in the REAL WORLD during school hours.  But it sure doesn't excite me like that day in the museum with Jesse, and I doubt those kids learned half so much about consumerism or the mathematics of money, as Jesse did counting out his own nickels and quarters and dimes and dollars.

### Approaching Math Through History

I'm wondering if any other homeschooling families have ever thought of the HISTORY of mathematics as being a source of possible interest to a non-math type of person (maybe you, or maybe your child), a way of beginning to look at mathematics in a new way with new eyes.  It's an approach we have always used around here with Jesse and Jacob, and I have learned so much right along with the kids.  Suddenly math, and even just "simple" arithmetic, becomes a long time-line of fascinating PEOPLE who tried, and tried hard, to make sense of their world with the best of their minds and the best tools of their times.   It's no longer just stuff put in textbooks and achievement tests.

We began very simply with books that talked about probable first uses of numbers -- cave men making drawings on cave walls to show how many elk they had caught, shepherds tallying up sheep as they ran through a primitive gate. (Once when Jesse was 6 or so he helped us tally up our sheep during some maneuver, and we were surprised to realize that -- with sheep running about -- tallying IS indeed the only way to count them.) We looked into other earlier number systems -- the Egyptian, the Babylonian, the Mayan, and the Roman systems. Many of these were actually much easier for young Jesse to grasp -- he seemed to have a mental block for a good while about our particular numeral system. Although he could THINK wonderfully well with numbers in his head, he just couldn't remember a written out "5" from an "8," let alone "6" and "9." I often thought how painful arithmetic in school would have been for him, with its emphasis on numeral recognition and good "penmanship" in writing those numerals. It was reassuring to him to find that many other peoples of the world, at different times, had come up with different inventions for writing down numbers -- our present system wasn't God-given and set for all time, but was just the latest in a long line of tries.

It's even been intriguing to learn about the history of standard math operation symbols. My kids were delighted to hear stories about how the "x" sign was first used for multiplication, and all the various ways used for a century or two to show decimal notation (and how the very idea of decimal notation at all was invented...). The equals sign ("=") has a history -- a certain mathematician felt it was the best symbol to use (others had been tried before him) because what could be more equal than two parallel lines. And there was quite a hullabaloo over how to write out fractions for a long time -- and we found that the Greeks didn't even want to consider fractions at all because they felt only the whole, natural numbers were perfect.

Now that Jesse is nine and Jacob is six, we've moved a bit farther in our math history. Jesse was just working on a section in his Miquon Math book (a workbook in a primary grade math series) introducing simple coordinate geometry -- and I can't understand why textbooks don't MENTION that these ideas have a STORY behind them, people who struggled to come up with these ideas. So we've just today read about Descartes and how he came up with his way of translating Euclid's geometry into algebra with his graphing system. Now we're not doing fabulously advanced work here, just graphing simple lines, but Jesse is grasping the idea that there is a lot more to it, that Descartes graphed circles and parabolas and ellipses, and that these methods paved the way for Newton to develop Calculus. Jesse isn't DOING calculus of course, but he's already hearing the word in non-scary contexts (we've just completed a good biography of Newton), as part of a STORY. I know when he comes to study it in later years that he'll immediately remember the good stories of Leibnitz and Newton's "feud" over who really invented the idea in the first place. The topic will have a context for him, a time frame, a hook to place it in history. It won't just be textbook stuff with no past, not just a dry present of abstract problems to complete.

We've read a bit about Archimedes and Euclid and Pythagorus and other early Greek mathematicians, finding out how the Greeks' unique world view helped them to make the discoveries they did. Studying Math history is indeed one of the fine ways to view history (maybe better than the war-rulers-vanquished approach) -- it is not separate from the rest of the problems, or ideals, of the people of its time. We love reading about Pythagorus and his mystic group of students inventing numerology lore along with their concrete discoveries about triangle and square numbers and prime numbers. We're touched reading about Archimedes asking a conquering Roman soldier, about to run him through with a sword, to please wait just a minute so that he could finish the geometrical proof he was working out in the sand with a pointed stick. And of course the kids love the story of Archimedes running through the city after his bath shouting "Eureka! Eureka!" and love hearing about his fabulous cranks and cranes that could lift enemy ships right out the water and shake all the sailors out into the harbor. And when Jesse and Jacob come to more formally study geometry at some point, they'll think of Euclid gathering together all the theorems and proofs of three centuries of Greek geometrical thought and organizing them into his 13 books. And they'll think of how Newton thought Euclid was just TOO obvious, and so he skirted over studying him thoroughly in favor of the more contemporary Descartes, only to be severely reprimanded by his mentor at Trinity College for this slighting. And of how when printing presses were first invented, Euclid's books were among the first to be published. Geometry won't just be some required course for some vague purpose like "getting into college," but a study tied to past stories (AND real experiences with compasses and rulers and blocks and hexagon tiles and all the geodesic models hanging from our ceiling).

And finding that early on Descartes and his mentor up in Holland tried to work out the solution to the problem of velocity of falling objects, not knowing that Galileo had just solved the problem down in Italy, let us see again what it might have been like to live in a world with slower communication systems than now, indeed with no real communication systems at all. Learning about math history doesn't keep just in the realm of math, but as John Holt often said of the serious historical study of ANYTHING, leads to wider understandings of all sorts.

A fine author about the history of mathematics is Morris Kline. He's written profusely -- *Mathematics and the Physical World* and *Why Johnny Can't Add* are two I've read so far. I hear he has a new one out now specifically written to the "layman" about math history. He firmly believes that it has been one of the disasters of the education system to abstract math away from its history and roots in the real world. To teach math as if it were devoid of human interest or growth or change, and not linked to real physical problems out there in the world. Kline points out in his books also how intuitive many of the first mathematical discoveries were -- an intuitive hunch, a wondering, a dream image, that only later (often much later) was codified and formally proven and turned pristine and clean and pure and theoretical and abstract. (Calculus was this way...

Newton couldn't "prove" formally why it worked.)  He feels, too, that perhaps children would learn mathematics best in the order in which it was invented, that this would be a more natural unfolding at a more relaxed pace.  And as for some of you folks who might be wondering, say, what good use negative numbers are, Kline would assure you that not only the "common folk" but even the greatest mathematicians of the day balked equally hard at the idea of negative numbers for centuries after they were first introduced from India.  (Seems in India, negative numbers were first used very concretely as a way of talking about debts.)  And the whole idea of irrational numbers so upset Pythagorus that he made all his students vow they would never tell anyone about these "unspeakables," these terrible blotches on his perfect number system -- and he surely wouldn't have liked the idea of negative numbers any better.  Kline says if it took the great mathematical thinkers of the world so long to feel comfortable with these ideas, we should at least be a bit patient and understanding when a kid today feels a bit anxious around them or wonders what good they are.

Jacob (6 1/2) is the one who is surprising me lately with his math ruminating.  Jacob is a daydreamy sort, who is often wandering about apparently doing "nothing."  He's now letting me in on his world a bit more, and more often than not, he's been wondering about some math pattern he's been playing around with in his mind.  Math thinking is indeed one of Jacob's favorite playthings.  He'll stumble (often literally, Jacob can bump and tumble over anything or nothing) into the kitchen to announce happily that he knows how many hundreds there are in 2000!  (I've checked the first grade "curriculum" for the district -- they aren't supposed to "get" to such big numbers until the next year...).  He relates that he knew there were ten hundreds in one thousand, so there must be 20 hundreds in two thousand.  Or I remember the time this last winter when we were driving home late at night from Pittsburgh and I was sure all the kids had peacefully fallen asleep in the back seat, and suddenly Jacob's shy voice pipes up out of the dark with, "Do you know that ten hundreds is the same as twenty 50's???" Or he's always coming up with theories about square numbers, trying to find patterns in them (often erroneous, but still showing good thought). I often wonder what a school would have done with Jacob -- he still writes numerals backwards as often as forwards. (Though with chalkboard work he's getting better at it, and getting proud about his ability rather than balky about even trying.) The type of problems he's interested in wouldn't come up in the usual first grade textbook, and daydreaming is rarely tolerated in schools, let alone encouraged. And of course he never would have let his teacher know that he was daydreaming about NUMBERS of all things.

Sometimes as we play with geoboards or Cuisenaire rods or geodesic building sets or seeing what patterns we can make with our compasses, I think how Archimedes might have loved to use such toys, such playthings. These great mathematicians indeed WERE playful it seems -- and perhaps that's one of the most important ideas I hope to pass on to my kids in our math history learnings...

### Starting Out With Cuisenaire Rods

Even before our children could recognize written numbers, they were discovering number concepts by, among other things in their world, using their Cuisenaire rods -- wooden blocks in 10 graduating sizes from a one centimeter cube to a 10 centimeter rod (1 x 1 x 10). You can build a "stairway" of rods from smallest to longest (see picture). Each length is always the same color -- red rods are always 2 cm.. long, blues are always 9 cm., etc. A small (74 rod) set of the rods runs about $7.[5] There are no markings or numerals on the rods, which makes them more flexible in actual use.

I own a large set of Cuisenaire rods left over from a summer program I'd worked with years ago. I originally wanted to order

---

[5]Available from Cuisenaire Co. of America, 12 Church St. -- Box D, New Rochelle, NY 10802, phone 800-237-3142.

them for the program because I'd read about them so much in John Holt's *How Children Fail* and *How Children Learn.* I couldn't figure out *what* in the world the rods looked like, and wanted to buy a set to find out. The kids I worked with that summer enjoyed making pretty patterns with the rods, but I never had a chance to see children really *use* the rods for mathematical purposes. One "open" first grade classroom I worked in while in college had Cuisenaire rods, but used them only for "color identification" exercises. The children were not allowed free access to them, and "real" math was done basically with standard workbooks. I wondered if my own children would extend the rods' possibilities, really use them for something more than just a pretty set of miniature blocks. (They *are* beautiful, I still find them a visual and tactile feast...)

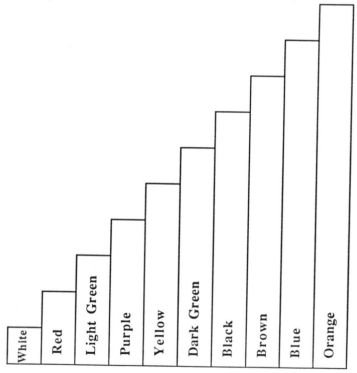

Jesse certainly spent a very long time building and playing freely with rods as a toddler and young child. All the time, though, he was learning about these lengths and their relationships. As a 2 1/2 year old, he'd figured out that all reds, say, were always the same size. He worked with great concentration paving rod "roads" of different widths, fitting in rods exactly. The rods became barns, trains, families. He discovered stairway patterns, and for a good while made lots of variations on these:

- What would happen if a yellow rod was added to each step?

- Could stairways go up and down?

- Could stairways be built on top of stairways?

We talked a lot about which rods were longer, which shorter, which ones when put together equaled others. Our language gradually came closer to that of mathematics. We talked of "Black minus purple equals light green," or "3 light greens equals 1 blue."

Although it's hard now to remember just when we began relating the rods to number ideas, I know we just very naturally began talking in "Cuisenaire" terms throughout the day. Lengths of objects became "Oh, that's about as long as a *purple*," or "I think my fingers are about a *black* long." This usually followed by testing out with actual rods. Once, when Jesse was asked to pick up 10 things from the kitchen floor, and he had found 5, we laughed about how he'd needed to find an *orange* worth of things, and had already found a *yellow*, another *yellow* to go. A dozen was referred to as an *orange* plus a *red*, or 2 *dark greens*, or 4 *light greens*, or 3 *purples*. Lots of talk of halves and quarters, while measuring whole wheat flour for baking, led us to look into these relationships in the rods -- could Jesse find half an *orange*, half a *purple*, half a *blue*? This was quite intriguing to Jesse, as he found that some rods didn't have even halves, and we began discussing ideas of odd and even numbers. Jesse made stairways of all odd rods and all even rods. We've examined thirds, quarters, fifths, sixths. We've even used rods on a simple balance scale, having fun with balancing different combinations of rods.

When Jesse was too young to comfortably use written numerals to keep score in games, we'd sometimes use rods as a graphic way to show the game's progress. I remember well the very first time we hit on this idea. Like many of our very best ideas, this one was NOT planned in advance! Instead, it was a response to a problem we were faced with. We'd made ourselves a set of American Indian stick "dice" and were trying to learn how to play some games of chance with them. A book we were using suggested a scoring system -- 4 points for one combination of sticks, 6 for another, 8 for another, 10 for another. We began to play, and I quickly saw that using numerals to keep score meant next to nothing to Jesse. The game seemed a bit pointless, but Jesse's Indian enthusiasm made us keep at it anyway.

Suddenly an idea flew in -- why not use our Cuisenaire rods for score keeping? We poured out all of our rods and set to. I told Jesse that we could use any combination of rods that would equal the same number of *whites* (1 cm.) as our scores. So a score of 4 might be made with either *whites*, 2 *reds*, 1 *light green*, plus 1 *white* or 1 *purple*. Jesse caught on immediately and with great delight. We each kept score by lining up our rods along our own edges of the table; we agreed that going the width and length of the table equaled winning, and then we kept on going until our rod lines met. Anytime we saw we could exchange two or more rods for one longer length, we did it, if we wanted. I kept my own second game score entirely in *yellow* rods. There was an energy in the game now, active thinking and figuring, and delight in the varied patterns we made. How much better than juggling numeral symbols that as yet had no meaning for Jesse.

Somehow I think it was important that we didn't let the rods become just props for other play. Although Jesse and Jacob both fantasized richly i[with] the rods, we didn't mix Cuisenaire rods in with Lincoln logs, say, or use them as people for Tonka trucks, or stir them in with sand for pretend witch's brew. They were always a bit special, used only in certain places, carefully picked up, kept in certain containers. We found it helpful to either use them on rectangular trays or on an old secondhand coffee table with a raised edge (it's now officially called our "Cuisenaire table"). This kept the rods in one place, not falling scattered about, and also gave the boys a firm edge to line rods up against. We literally never put them away anymore, but always have them out ready for a moments use.

Once Jesse figured out how to show 100 with rods (10 *oranges*). Then he wanted to try to show one thousand. This took lots of work, as our set only has about 17 *oranges*. He worked very systematically and diligently -- the "200" square was made of all *yellow* rods (2 yellows equals 1 *orange*, the "300" square was made from 10 *blacks*, and 10 *light greens*, etc. These larger numbers have taken on quite a reality for Jesse. It reminds me of an experience I had as a 6 year old. I was lying in bed one night, counting as high as I could. I reached 100. Unsure what came next, I began saying "200, 300, 400, 500..." I stopped quickly, almost heady with the thought of how high I'd gone, but sensing that perhaps something might be wrong. But I had no way to test out my counting ideas, no model of how these bigger numbers really "worked." Jesse has rods to give him a very concrete way of imagining them.

Jesse seemed to really need, as well as enjoy, the concreteness of the rods. Written numerals meant little to him before almost age 6, even though we came upon numerals frequently on clocks, calendars, store advertisements, in books and games. The wiggles on paper just didn't carry meanings for him like the rods that he could tangibly feel and compare. With rods, addition combinations, say, are known by long experience and feel. They are all interrelated, observable, and real, rather than "math facts" to be memorized and drilled. I was amazed that the very first time Jesse saw written down addition problems this fall, he had absolutely no difficulty. I'd made a simple addition "concentration" game -- "1+5" could be matched to "3+3," or "2+4," or "5+1," or "6+0," etc. Jesse thought it was great fun, suggested other combinations I hadn't thought of. "Why couldn't you put '1+1+1' for 3?" etc. He lined up the cards in order, like he's done with rods, made a new game of adding up the *columns* of numbers, got out his rods to help him check his answers. The symbols are now easily understood and given meaning -- he is ready to transfer his very concrete ideas of number to numerical abstractions.

I can see that the rods have given Jesse, and now also Jacob, a very flexible approach to mathematics. Number ideas are playthings, delights, intriguing puzzles that fit together in ever varying new patterns. Mathematics is no dull workbook activity separate from his real living.

**Doing Math Work**

I was recently asked by some homeschooling mothers if Jesse, now 8 1/2, actually did math work readily, ALL ON HIS OWN, or did I have to force him to do it. I was a bit taken aback, and felt at a loss to answer. The question seemed too black/white, either/or, this/that. I had images of either complete abandonment (magically, some probably secretly hoping, creating a child who just LOVES math workbooks...) or a frantic, frazzled mother nailing her child to the dining room chair yelling "Do these ten multiplication problems OR ELSE!!!" To say Jesse goes to his math work ALL on his own completely by his own decision, seems an over-simplification of things. I've played a major role in helping Jesse see what math work might be appropriate, interesting and useful, and I keep a guiding, responsive hand in things. On the other hand, I don't need to yell or threaten or force, or even cajole him into his mathematics work. I'm trying here to sort out how this has come about.

Jesse, I think, knows several things about my views of mathematics. First, he knows it's an area I like and enjoy. I sometimes read books about math for my own pleasure (oh, not all the time, mind you, but a bit here and there), and I share good information I find with him. He also knows I sometimes leaf through some of the MANY books we have on math for kids and end up doing little geometric experiments, number line patterns, or puzzles myself -- just because I get inspired and intrigued by my reading. I've made paper models of pyramids, icosohedrons, cubes, and tetrahedrons. They know if I see a hexagon patterned sidewalk that I'm sure to remark enthusiastically about it. They also know that I snatch up geometric shaped paper-weights at any garage sale, and try to mentally figure out how to build models of "geodesic" shapes we come across. (We all especially got excited by the large cement geodesic banister heads outside the Capitol building in Harrisburg last time we were there lobbying for the Home Education Bill.) They know I've made our own geo-boards (square pieces of plywood with an evenly spaced array of nails dotting the surface -- you stretch rubber bands on to make all types of geometric patterns, show area, perimeter, you name it). I've spent time making our own Tangrams set out of wood (it's an old Chinese geometric puzzle, great fun for all ages). And my kids know that somehow I think Cuisenaire rods are important enough to warrant having their very own special table. It's always a sure thing that I'll buy games like "Quinto," or "Racko," or "Create a Cube," or one more set of dominoes at a yard sale, too. They don't think it's odd or suspicious for me to give them Tri-man protractors and compasses as little Christmas gifts, and they are always thrilled to get new tape measures or folding rulers.

And STILL, with all this good mathematical "stuff" in the atmosphere, we also do use official math work books. Not the school's third grade text that we borrowed this year -- it was so deadly and boring and repetitive we could barely stand to flip through it. It seemed to shout out that kids have no minds, and only need rote, rote, rote, in exactly the same format day after day after day. We've chosen the *Miquon Mathlab Materials*.[6]

---

[6]Available from Key Curriculum Project, P.O Box 2304-C, Berkeley, CA 94702, phone 800-338- 7638.

(The books are a good buy -- for less than $30.00 you get 3 teacher's guide books and 6 workbooks, roughly geared towards first through third grades, but really more advanced.) These books aren't "fancy" -- they don't try to rely on colorful, jazzy illustrations (usually totally un-related to the math work) like the school text we abandoned. The math is sound and CREATIVE, respecting the fact that children are curious, active learners and like to see pattern in the world about them. Lots of work helping kids see the rhythms of numbers and measurement. Also lots of places where kids are asked to make up their own problems ("How many different names can you think up for the number 27?" etc.). The books also use Cuisenaire rods regularly in modeling new processes, so they were a natural for us.

Now -- how does Jesse use these books? At times we've used them just as another resource, one choice among many. Jesse would dip into them as he pleased, not worrying about doing the work in "order." This was fine for a while, but left him unable to understand some ideas that had been built up over time. Sometimes I'd suggest specific pages to him, either because I thought he'd find them especially intriguing or because they covered something I felt he ought to be learning something about.

At first we didn't notice or use a nice feature about the books. There's a chart on the back cover listing all the pages in the book by categories -- multiplication, addition, inequalities, fractions, mapping, etc., with little boxes for each page number. I realized that Jesse might work with more concentration in the books if he could mark in on the chart which pages he'd completed. It would be a way for him to keep track of his own progress, give him a graphic picture of where he'd been and was going, and what to expect ahead. Using the charts has been a real turn-around. Jesse loves seeing the boxes get filled in, even began inventing little games about armies advancing and conquering all the new territories, as his yellow crayon filled in the boxes for pages completed. We also began setting goals -- I asked Jesse when he hoped to have one book completed, and then to figure out how many pages he'd need to complete daily (not counting weekends) to reach his goal. For the third book Jesse set March 1st as his completion goal, found he'd need to do two pages a day for the next month and a half to finish up -- and then proceeded to choose ON HIS OWN to work even on weekends so that he'd surprise us all by finishing up early! He sometimes decides to do more than two pages if he gets particularly excited by something, but doesn't use that as a reason to not do math work the next day, although he knows that would be OK by me.

When Jesse completed his book two weeks early he immediately wanted to dive into the next, and is now zooming along in the fourth book (correction -- as I'm retyping this he's finished the fourth book, early, and has begun the fifth...). He is still free to choose which sections of the books he works in, although he is now very diligent about being thorough and doing everything eventually. He explains that these out of sequence blocks on his chart are surprise raids into enemy territory -- we've been reading lots of books about the Civil War lately, so you'll have to excuse the battle imagery! I do think that his "playing" with the chart shows that he's found a way, on his own, to transform what might have been dull work into quite exciting play -- and his play makes the work his own.

Carol Wilson tells me her son, Luke, also enjoys this goal setting, chart-filling with the *Miquon* books. They seem to like, perhaps, having everything out in the open, a clear agenda they can understand, and have a share in shaping and pacing. I know, too, it helps Jesse to know that a number of our homeschooling friends also use these books. He likes hearing how other kids are doing with them, makes it all into a sort of social experience.

I am usually closely involved and in touch with what Jesse is doing with these books. I'm nearby, ready to offer help as needed, ready to share in discoveries and connections he's making. Ready to help him over or around a snarl or frustration that may come up. And I usually enjoy the subject, and make my own new connections, too. I had my "come-uppance" on this recently. I was heading out to milk the goats with two year old

Molly, while Jesse and Jacob chose to stay inside. Jesse had decided he'd work in his math book while I was gone. As I left I thought to myself, "Ah! He's finally getting more independent in his math work -- terrific!" When I returned I tried to glance over what he'd done, feeling, as teachers in schools must, that since I hadn't been there to see his process of work and thinking, I must now check up afterwards to see if he'd done it all "right." I quickly saw a few gross errors, and tried to question Jesse about them, and "help" him. His reaction was to try to physically cover the page with his arms, and then even grab the book away from me. He became furious with me, and finally burst out, in choked tears, that if I wasn't going to be there while he was doing something, then I had no right to say anything about it afterwards. SO -- I now try to always be physically nearby, present in all ways, as he's doing math, discussing the work with him as he chooses, and Jesse's much happier for it. There's more of a sense of camaraderie about the work -- we are more like colleagues, out of the roles of task-master/ child-academic slave, and onto both being students, ready to learn from the situation. He can sense more concretely my respect for his growing and his emerging ideas. I've responded to HIM.

But what do Jacob, just 5 1/2, and Molly 2 1/2, do while I'm helping Jesse with math? All depends. Mostly Molly is sitting on my lap (and, yes, sometimes kicking at Jesse's math book with a chubby, well-aimed foot). On some days, perhaps the best days, I get out manipulative math materials for Jacob and Molly -- cubical blocks, sum-stick, geoboards, puzzles, counting games, dice, etc., and they use these on the floor nearby while Jesse works at his desk. We actually do have old school desks for each of the boys -- yard sale finds again. I used to be perhaps "philosophically opposed" to having official desks for the kids, but have found that having a work surface to call your own, that's the right height for you, where you can store all sorts of books and treasures is good for the kids and they love their desk areas. Molly is clamoring for one too.

One day Jacob and Molly both happened to be building

bigger and bigger sized squares with various tiles and blocks --
while Jesse was working on several pages dealing with square
numbers! I was quick to point out the tie-in. Feels good when
we can all be working in the same basic area at the same time,
each in our own ways.

I think, too, that Jacob is less interruptive to Jesse's work if
he's also had some good one-on-one time with me, if it doesn't
seem like I'm just always pushing him aside or telling him to be
quiet so I can do REAL work with Jesse. Jacob appreciates it
when I won't let Jesse bother US when we are doing something
special together. And Jesse needing me nearby doesn't mean he
needs me ogling over his shoulder every second. I don't need to
give him every bit of my attention. It's often enough that I keep
in touch, discussing his work with him in between responding to
Molly or Jacob, or in between sweeping the project room floor.
Also Jacob and even Molly are now used to Jesse spending some
time each day doing math work. They expect these shifts in
work and play just as much as Jesse, and so don't balk (much) at
them. Jacob is gradually working into a math time for himself --
sometimes using simple workbooks, or his own calculator, or
Cuisenaire rods. And it's not odd now for Jacob to go about the
house wondering aloud if two odd numbers added together will
give you an odd or an even number for an answer, or coming up
with a "tricky problem" for Jesse to solve.

Sometimes, of course, Molly is tired, hungry, or just plain out
of sorts (maybe even rolling on the floor kicking and screaming
after Jesse has yelled at her for knocking his carefully arranged
Cuisenaire rods off his desk and all over the floor...). Then the
most helpful thing I can do for everyone is to physically take
Molly from the scene and calm her down somewhere else. Let
her help me wash dishes in the sink (ah, water, the great
soother...) get her a snack, get her a nap up in the bedroom where
it's quiet. Jesse and Jacob both understand, then, that I can't be
available to them for a bit. We're all gradually learning the
balancing act of living with a passionate little person who wants
to be in on EVERYTHING. Not always easy, but very exciting

to see how she's growing and learning too. The other day during Jesse's math time she spent at least half an hour stretching rubber bands very carefully on a geoboard, then watching to see if I could duplicate what she had done on my larger board. She made purposeful patterns -- little squares next to big ones (Mommy squares with their baby squares, she said...), triangles stretching magically into rectangles. She also loves our Cuisenaire rods, lines them up in rows and patterns, and never even TRIES to eat them. Molly even sometimes wants to do "her" workbooks, meaning she wants to scribble all over the pages of an old free workbook we picked up somewhere. So even her math time is coming along too.

One other thing about Jesse and math -- he has an important math JOB in our family. He's the official treasurer for our newsletter, and is in charge of filling out deposit slips for our newsletter checking account. Lots of real adding and multiplying here and a real need for accuracy. (He now readily accepts the idea of checking over his calculations, since we once received a notice from the bank saying that we actually had deposited $8.00 more than Jesse had recorded on the slip!) Jesse takes on this work seriously and very happily, feeling very adult (for me it was pure drudgery and I couldn't stand doing it, "red tape" never being my forte). This work has also brought about many good discussions of how checking accounts really work, how banks function, why forms are made as they are, etc. I'd urge any homeschooling family to consider giving a child a real family job that uses math calculating as part of it. I know that Barbara McMillan mentioned once that when her family went on long trips, Jaime's job was figuring out total mileage and how much was spent on gas. Kids could help pay bills or balance check-books. The possibilities are endless, and what may seem like boring routine paperwork for us, may be an exciting in-road into the adult world for our children.

So, I don't think our math work at home is coerced or narrow, but neither is it totally "free form" in the sense of having no guidance from me. I've helped set a "math appreciation" atmosphere just as many parents actively create a rich musical atmosphere in their homes. I've worked to help the kids feel that it's just an expected tradition that we do some math work each day, just in the same way that, say, we eat three regular meals. And, like our meals that we all share together and have a good time at, so too we're sharing together in these math times. Rather than it being a fight for me to force the kids to "do their math work or else," we're ALL taking part, ALL learning, and ALL in it together. Makes a difference.

### Using a Math Textbook

I have taught myself simple statistics and three computer languages by working through beginning textbooks. In each case, I had a real reason for learning what the textbook had to offer. I had a problem that I wanted to solve, and the textbook enabled me to learn what I needed to know in order to solve the problem.

I once saw a television interview (the "Nova" show on public television) with one of the most famous physicists of our time, Richard Feynman. He described how he had learned calculus as a young boy. He had gone to the library and picked out *Calculus for the Practical Man.* When he took it to the checkout counter, the librarian challenged him. "Why are you taking out this book?" and Feynman lied, thinking the librarian wouldn't believe that he was taking it out for himself, "I'm taking it out for my father!" Later, on the recommendation of his high school physics teacher Feynman worked through an advanced calculus textbook on his own which gave him a slightly different knowledge of calculus than that of his fellow physicists. Later, he would often be able to solve equations that stumped everyone else, not because he knew a better way, but because he knew a different way.

The math textbooks written by John Saxon have been a favorite with many homeschoolers. Jesse is just starting to use *Math 76* (for sixth or seventh graders) which Saxon wrote

**with Stephen Hake.**[7]  In issue number 20 of *Pennsylvania Homeschoolers*, Nathan Williamson, a ten year old homeschooled boy wrote:

> There are many math books. They all have math in them. But the one I like is Saxon Math. I like the way Saxon Math programs the lessons and the problems so I can find where I'm at. I was never good in math. I was nine and I was in third grade math. But now I'm ten and I'm doing sixth grade math. And I feel good about me!

Textbooks -- many of us use them, but sometimes we feel "guilty" about using or over-using them.  Guilty that we are turning our homes into miniature schools of just the sort we've always complained about.  Sometimes we may forget that we do have freedom -- we can USE these books HOW we want to. They can be our resources, helps, references, idea starters -- they don't have to be the end all and be all that they so often are in schools.

We use a math textbook with Jesse, always have, but I'm so glad we are free to use it as WE see fit, and not feel we need to slavishly follow it problem for problem without thought.  I always feel it's most useful to us when we use it as a springboard to other real life math problems -- problems WE want to solve and work on.

A few days ago Jesse noticed that the next section in the text was on reading different types of graphs, something that has always been easy for him.  He said right off, "Oh, I know they always have reading graphs on achievement tests," meaning that he therefore wanted to work on them a bit so he'd be all set.

But the graphs were so insipid, so downright stupid.  Graphs of how imaginary students in a fifth grade class got to school (bicycle, walk, or bus), graphs of the favorite colors of 5th and 6th grade students, graphs of heights of Leo, Pam, Rob, Kim, and Jay (pretend members of a pretend 5th grade class).  A few

---

[7]Available from Saxon Publishers Inc., 1002 Lincoln Green, Norman, Oklahoma 73069.

were a touch more intriguing -- a graph of the growth of a baby mouse, or graphs of breathing rate and pulse rate after exercise.

But they just were not something we could exactly sink our teeth into. And I realized that we didn't HAVE to feel bound at all to doing work with these contrived graphs -- Jesse could make his own on a topic of interest to him. He could graph something he wanted to find out about, and possibly see how graphs actually are useful in sorting out information.

That same day we somehow stumbled into rummaging through our Almanac, something both boys really enjoy. I can't even remember now quite how it got started, but soon we were looking for answers to questions we had about the U.S. Census, and soon Jesse was grabbing the book and pouring over all the charts and tables about population growth in the U.S. Much more complex chart reading here than his math text offered -- and here we knew the statistics were REAL (we have our doubts about the accuracy of the math book problems -- sometimes we've felt burned when we've found that their "statistics" were totally made up and phony).

I told Jesse that his challenge was to make a graph using any of the information he found in the Almanac to make his own bar graph. He chose to show the changes of population in the original thirteen states from 1790 (the time of the first census) to 1900.

In an hour he was done -- and proud! And I think he learned MUCH more than he would have had he studiously completed the entire chapter in the text about graphing. He had to decipher charts and tables of statistics, and sort out what information was relevant to his chosen topic. Then he had to decide on a format to use -- where to list the states, where to list the populations, how to differentiate between the 1790 and the 1900 statistics, how to set a reasonable scale (not so large that he'd need three sheets of paper to show his results, not so small that the graph would take up only 4 tiny blocks on his graph paper...), and more.

And the most valuable lesson came as he was actually filling in the blocks with yellow and blue -- he began realizing with excitement how a graph really SHOWS information in a new way. As Jacob said while watching it all, "Just reading it in a table in the Almanac doesn't let you SEE it all at once." The graph gave him a picture (isn't that what "graph" means anyway?) of his results, and he marveled over his new findings for a good while. "Hey, look, you can just SEE that New York really took off, but Virginia sure lost its place as number one," and "Now you can see why I needed to go all the way up to 7 million," and "Just look how some states hardly grew at ALL."

The idea has really taken off, and Jesse has now made several more graphs, all with the same enthusiasm. He's graphed the population growth of Pennsylvania from 1790 to the present, showing the population recorded by every census. He then made a graph of Georgia's and Florida's growth, careful to use the same scale as his Pennsylvania graph so he could really compare results. He's pored over these growth curves with a historian's eye, wondering why certain times saw large boosts in population, why other times growth slowed down.

He also made a very useful graph of new and renewal subscriptions to *PA Homeschoolers*, using data collected over the last two years. He already handles the checking account deposits, so this was a natural for him.

Now in all honesty, I probably wouldn't have thought of the idea of suggesting Jesse make his own graphs if there hadn't been that graphing unit in Jesse's book. That was the good use of the book. It got an idea going. So glad we let the math text book be a leaping off place today.

## Math in the Real World

We're finding out more and more that all branches of math that we've studied don't just stay textbook problems for us. We're beginning to see the math that surrounds us all the while, and Jesse's growing ability and understanding of arithmetic is helping him do more with the real world.

We recently took a family trip all through the Southeast of our country, and "math" took place every day. Jesse and Jacob were often our navigators, and often estimated how long a certain drive should take -- which meant adding up mileage and figuring out the maps' scale, then figuring how fast we were driving, then allowing in for stops for meals or rest stops. Or Jesse figured out the average price of meals -- he'd heard endless discussions about the relative prices of steak houses and salad bars and fast food joints!

We saw the Gateway Arch Monument in St. Louis and talked and read about catenary arches and the types of curves made when you suspend a chain from two points, and saw how the whole arch was made up of gently decreasing equilateral triangles. We also felt first hand the full 18 inches of allowable "sway" to the arch as we looked over the city of St. Louis on that VERY windy day! We tried to mentally calculate if the Arch was as tall as the US Steel Building in Pittsburgh.

On one of our last days on the road, Jesse figured out the average distance we'd travelled each day -- and could also see how meaningless such an average could be. "One hundred miles a day" was the proper answer to the problem, but that told nothing about the six or seven hours pushing for as many miles as possible one day, versus a quick half hour out to a beach another. (I used the chance to mention how so MANY averages mean just as little -- the *TELLS* test "average score" for the whole state of Pennsylvania tells us nothing at all about any individual child's actual score.)

**Math in Real Books**

Speaking of averages, Jesse recently read with great delight a book called *What Do You Mean by Average?*, about a girl who was trying to win a school election campaign with the slogan that she was the "average" girl in every way. The book brings in all the different ways to calculate averages, and how they all tell us different sorts of things. The book was a far cry from a math textbook -- it's amazing how many good math books there are to READ. And amazing how if an idea is tied to a STORY, then the idea sinks in and is remembered.

We also had enormous math fun recently with a Newberry Award book, *The Phantom Tollbooth*, by Norman Juster. I'd owned the book for years but we'd never opened it until I realized the same author had written the delightful math fantasy picture book, *The Dot and the Line* (another math must). The book's basic plot is a sort of *Alice in Wonderland* journey to free two princesses ("Rhyme" and "Reason"), and at one point the young hero must travel through Digitopolis, the Kingdom of Numbers. Here we met a Dodecahedron character, who appropriately enough had ten FACES on his geometric head (we all made our own paper models of dodecahedrons with a different face drawing on each "face" of the solid -- don't think they'll ever get mixed up on what that math term means!) The Dodecahedron spouted out such problems as:

> Why, did you know that if a beaver two feet long with a tail a foot and a half long can build a dam twelve feet high and six feet wide in two days, all you would need to build Boulder Dam is a beaver sixty-eight feet long with a fifty-one-foot tail?[13]

This reminded us of the funny Mark Twain story about how "useful" mathematics was -- why, with mathematics, you could show that the Mississippi River was losing so much length each year by meanders straightening out in flood time, that by the year 1927 the Mississippi River would be only 2.5 miles long from headwaters to mouth! (We thought of this as we gazed at the river on our trip, too)

Jesse also came upon the notion of the absurdity of some ideas of "average" in the PHANTOM TOLLBOOTH when meeting the boy in the story who was only half there, cut right down the middle. Or, to put it more exactly, cut into .58 of a child, for he was the extra bit of a child from the average size family with "2.58 children." If your child finds all math ideas terribly serious and dull and tedious, try this book out on him!

Another book that gave the kids a real laugh AND some new mathematics thinking, was Mitsumasa Anno's book *Socrates and the Three Little Pigs*, a book about permutations and probability. This one is not a wordless picture book like many of Anno's, but has a delightful text following the thinking of the wolf, Socrates, as he tries to decide which house would be the most likely to have a little pig in it. Quite sophisticated math, done very graphically -- and with fine humor. We also are enjoying Anno's book *Sundials*, which goes into all the mathematics of time-telling, with the earth envisioned as a big sundial. Longitude, latitude, the movements and angles of shadows all become real things to experiment with. The book even has pop-up sundials all through it. (We keep this one away from Baby Hannah!)

Once you begin opening up to the world of math all around you, I guarantee that good books and resources and "natural" problems will spring up at you. Carl Sandburg even wrote poems about math, and most folks know that Lewis Caroll was not primarily a children's author, but was actually a mathematician. You'll be able to extend the textbook learnings into reality. Why, I've been amazed to find that even multiplication of fractions ACTUALLY happens -- it's not just something to plague fifth grade math students.

# 9. Tests and Records

One of the nicest things about helping our own kids learn to read at home is that we are free to NOT submit them to COMPREHENSION exercises when they read. Our kids do not view reading as an exercise in reading a boring paragraph in order to answer the five boring multiple choice questions at the end. They don't have quizzes to make sure they actually read the material assigned to them -- and I frankly never "assign" reading material, either. (I remember an English teacher in high school wistfully saying that he WISHED he didn't have to give these silly quizzes, but he'd found that no one would actually read the assigned books if he didn't.) Our kids don't do workbook drill on finding the main idea, or recognizing sequence, or getting meaning from context, or any other very official sounding "comprehension skills."

So what do we do instead? Well, we read together, and we talk a lot about what we read. We ALL bring up questions, we all wonder about the meanings of specific words, we all look up words together in dictionaries, we all make conjectures about outcomes, we all talk about who book characters remind us of. In short, we RESPOND to real literature, to anything we read, and we share our responses. And because the kids choose their own books (with suggestions from me, of course), they really read them for their own purposes. They are even free to stop reading a book if it really doesn't appeal to them after a bit -- a freedom most schools using a basal reading system just can't give.

Often times Jesse, now ten, reads books that I've recommended because I've read them before, maybe twelve years before in a children's literature course in college. He usually dives right in, perhaps because he knows I've given some decent advice about books in the past.   Soon he is immersed in, say, *The Witch of Blackbird Pond.*  He's off by himself, curled up on the livingroom sofa, oblivious to the world, while I'm maybe busy doing more mundane things like washing dishes.

So how do I know he's "getting" this mature book with any understanding?   First, I assume he wouldn't keep at it if he weren't getting something out of it.  As John Holt liked to say, kids just don't suck at dry straws.

And I ask Jesse questions about the book.  I don't look to a list of ten "canned" comprehension questions to check up on his reading, but I do question him.  My questions spring from my genuine wonderings -- it's actually a HELP here to our conversations that I so often forget the details of a particular story.  "Hey, Jess, isn't the main character in *Witch of Blackbird Pond* originally from some other place, some island somewhere? Somewhere with a very different lifestyle?"  And so he tells me all about Kit being brought to New England from Barbados, and how much trouble she has fitting in.  And I may dimly remember that the title of the book has some other meanings, and ask Jesse what he thinks of it, and he tells me about the Quaker woman, the "witch" whom Kit visits.  The whole tone would be different if he sensed I was just checking up on him, just nervously assessing his "skills."   Instead we are discussing, sharing something together, both curious and alive to what the book can tell us.  We are colleagues together.

The same thing can happen even if I haven't previously read a book that Jesse chooses.  Maybe I'm like a newspaper reporter interviewing him about a book, as if it is an event he's witnessed that I want to find out about.  He's the assumed expert, as HE'S read it, and I find I naturally have lots of questions for him:

- What type of book is it?

- Does it remind him of any others he's read?

- What does the title seem to mean?

- Is it told in the first person or the third?

- Does he think we should buy it for our home library, or recommend it to anyone else, is it THAT good?

- Is it like other books by the same author?

I'm not like an examiner, I'm just really wondering about this new friend of a book he's met.

And often Jacob, age seven, overhears these conversations. And then he begins clamoring for us to read Jesse's book as our next read-aloud. And so we ALL got to share in *Tom Sawyer* and *Huckleberry Finn* this past Fall -- the books didn't just stay Jesse's sole property. Interestingly, Jesse told me several times that HE really enjoyed it when I read aloud these books he'd already been through, found he got even more out of them the second time around, was able to pay attention to other things besides just figuring out the story line. This shared reading also gave us a chance to look up intriguing words in the dictionary together -- and *Tom Sawyer* especially held a number that I wasn't quite sure of. The dictionary became a tool for better comprehension right in its proper context -- while actually reading and wondering about meanings. We had a chance to naturally discuss the book's themes and ideas and characters, again being colleagues discovering a book together.

Jacob is now delighting in reading all of Arnold Lobel's easy reading books -- *Frog and Toad, Mouse Tales, Uncle Elephant, Owl at Home,* and others. These are stories he already knows and loves, because I've read them aloud MANY times. How different from reading a basal reading "story" in school, a story that the teacher is scrupulously certain no one has laid eyes on before. (You have all probably heard the stories of the bright child in first grade who gets in trouble because he has READ AHEAD in the reader...) The classroom teacher is ideally supposed to ask a number of leading questions of the circle of kids around her, questions to get them imagining what might happen in this unknown story, then questions to check up on how well they figured out what actually did happen, with perhaps a

question or two about why it all happened. Sometimes it's even
recommended that the kids have a sheet of paper to cover over
the next part of the story so they don't get ahead during the
lesson!

Well, I obviously can't do that with Jacob -- he already
knows the story. So we skip all the questioning and are left with
reading's REAL delight -- savoring a good story. We get to just
laugh, just enjoy, just remember again how funny a certain story
was. Oh, sometimes I "pretend" to ask Jacob questions about
what he thinks will happen next, pretending I can't remember the
story's events, but he knows I'm pretending and that maybe
together we're pretending that we're reading it all for the first
time. And to Jacob that just makes the story become even
funnier.

Now, I don't think you could do this with a story that wasn't
already a fine story -- re-reading demands quality. (Is THAT
why the schools don't want the kids reading ahead in their
official readers -- they might never be able to hood-wink the
poor students into reading the meager stories a second time
through?) Wooden writing won't do. Shabby illustrations won't
do. Lack of character and humaneness and pathos and humor
won't do. But Jacob has found Arnold Lobel, and who could be
more wonderful?

Oddly enough, when the kids are faced with the usual
comprehension drivel each year on achievement tests -- those
boring paragraphs followed by the multiple choice questions that
kids in most schools plow through on a daily basis -- they do just
fine. Jesse now scores way above grade level in reading. The
"personalized" computer print- out on his achievement test
results even kindly suggest I ask his teacher(!?!) to consider
planning advanced supplementary work, as Jesse has already
mastered all the skills expected for his grade level and then
some. We do do a touch of preparation for these tests -- a few
look-overs of sample test paragraphs and questions just so he
will know the format of these types of tests. We talk a bit about
"trick" types of questions, or strategies of sometimes glancing

over the questions first before hitting the paragraph, or the need to keep moving quickly and not get bogged down in any one section. And he gets everything correct -- no "comprehension problem" at all.

Perhaps Jesse does well in testing in part because he is not "burnt out" on comprehension exercises. To my kids, these tests are like a novel game that we only play once or twice a year, and it's a touch intriguing for them to see how they can do. They know my feelings about these tests, but they also understand that it's part of a game they need to learn to play. And loving reading, reading widely, and having someone to talk to about your responses to books seem to actually be the best preparation of all for these tests.

Interesting to remember, too, that these reading comprehension tests were originally designed just to quickly assess a child's rough reading ability. The short paragraphs of increasing difficulty -- and the boring questions -- were never meant as a model of what kids should be doing as their daily fare in school. It's another example of the test becoming the teaching method. We don't have to fall for that at home. Let's let our kids really read.

## Homeschooled Children Score High

According to test results, homeschooled children generally score higher on standardized achievement tests than school educated children. So far, every state that tests homeschooled children has reported that, as a group, they are doing average or better. The most thorough study of homeschooled children's test scores was conducted by Jon Wartes and the Washington Homeschool Research Project. They had access to the test scores of all of the children who were homeschooling under the present friendly homeschooling law in Washington State. They found that, as a group, homeschooled children score well above average (median scores in the 65 to 68 percentile range). Homeschooled children scored particularly well in Listening, Vocabulary, and Word Reading, but lower in Math. Still, the average Math scores were above the national norm. Even children of parents who only have a 12th grade education scored, as a group, above average.[14]

What do these test scores mean?

- Do they mean that home-education is more effective than school education?  Not necessarily. It is quite possible that home-educated children would also do better than average if they were attending school.   Research shows that, in general, children who are read to at home do better than average in school.

- Do they mean that every home-educated child will score better than average on achievement tests?    Not    necessarily.    Even    though homeschooled children, as a group, score well on achievement tests, not every homeschooled child will   score   above   average.    First,   not   all homeschooled children start to read as early as children start to read in schools. These children will not be able to score well on tests until they become readers.  Also not every child is above average.    Many   parents   are   teaching   their children at home because they know that unique qualities of their children would prevent them from doing well in schools.

Nevertheless, in many states, the establishment requires home-schooled children to score well on tests or risk losing permission to continue homeschooling.   As a result, homeschooling families find that they must prepare their children for taking standardized achievement tests.

## Preparing for Standardized Tests

Most homeschooled children are faced at some time with standardized achievement tests, and parents wonder about how best to prepare their kids. The natural urge to help their kids have a positive experience is often coupled with anxiety, as parents are often told right out that their kids scores will be a chief determiner in deciding if the family can continue homeschooling.

It is interesting that tests *are* different, and parents really should ask to see exactly what skills are being looked at. I just looked over a 4th grade Stanford Achievement Test, and was surprised to see two pages devoted to choosing the correct syllabication of a given word. The 4th grade California Achievement Test has nothing on this "skill," it's not even mentioned once anywhere on the test.

Another difference: the Metropolitan and the Stanford both have social studies and science sections at the first and second grade levels, involving no reading at all, just picking out the right picture to answer the question. Some other tests seem to just focus on the "basics" for the first grade levels and just test math and reading skills. I was always glad that Jesse had his science and social studies scores (very high, top of the test) to balance out his 4th percentile reading score in first grade. His results in these other areas could show that he was a well-rounded kid who seemed to know a lot about the world and how it worked, even if he was just a beginning reader.

Then some tests (Metropolitan and California are two) face the child with reading paragraphs that go way beyond the child's grade level -- up to official fifth grade reading paragraphs for a first grader's test. The Stanford seems to just give a child a whole bunch of (usually shorter) paragraphs right on the child's expected grade level, or maybe one level higher. So the Met and the CAT would benefit a child who reads way above grade level, because he or she would be able to *show* something, but the poor kid who is just doing fine would feel like a failure when faced with half a dozen paragraphs and what seem like zillions of

questions that are clearly too hard.  The Stanford might be better
for not intimidating a slow reader.

I also heartily recommend the *Scoring High* test preparation
books published by Random House.[8]  They really mimic the
actual tests, helping our kids feel more comfortable in a
standardized testing situation.  I think doing too much of this
kind of practice could be worse than a mere "drag," but a little
bit can help a lot in letting a child (and parent) know what to
expect.  I know this spring Jesse really appreciated the chance to
try out in advance what it would be like to use a separate
computer answer sheet.  (Before fourth grade, students usually
mark their answers right in the test booklet.)  If we can help
make as many things as possible not totally new and therefore
stressful, all the better.  It was also useful for Jesse to try timing
himself on sections of the practice test, as this is certainly
something we don't do at all at home.

I remember one year in high school taking an official IQ test
-- one of those affairs where hundreds and hundreds of students
were sitting at those awful "elbow" desks spread in rows and
columns in the school gymnasium, with instructions read over
the loudspeaker system.  I remember being pleasantly surprised,
even delighted, by the test.   Why, it was actually full of
intriguing puzzles and brain-teasers, the sort of thing you might
even choose to do on your own on a rainy day inside.  Lots of
visual puzzles of the type, "All of these shapes are *bleeps*, which
of the next group of shapes is *not a bleep*?"  Being a visually
oriented kid, this was a delightful change from the usual verbal,
read a boring paragraph and answer the three boring questions
test.  I was readily imagining to myself how *well* I must be
doing, how high my IQ must be.  But then, somehow, I happened
to glance over at Michael Wolfe's answer sheet in the next row.
Now, I wasn't the cheating type, and anyway he was too far
away for me to actually see any of the answers he'd fill in on his

[9]Available from *PA Homeschoolers*, RD2 -- Box 117, Kittanning
PA 16201, 412-783-6512.

computer answer sheet.  What I did see that shook me was that he was at least 60 or so questions *ahead* of me, and I knew this kid was not as "bright" and certainly not as flexible a thinker as I fancied myself to be.  It suddenly hit me like an iron weight that the test makers had not been trying to find a way for me to have a jolly two hours in the school gym doing delightful mental acrobatics.  They were *testing* me.  They didn't care about my almost laughing aloud when I discovered a solution to one of their problems.  They cared only about right answers, and not only that, they cared only about my *speed* in marking those answers down on an answer sheet.  I was using a bad "test taking strategy" to be taking time to savor and chuckle over some of the "good" questions, as you could readily do curled up with a book of brain teasers at home in the rainy day scenario.  This was a test scenario.  I remember then feeling only stressed by the test, all sense of fun stolen...

### Jesse's Experience With Tests

I went to our school district to begin working out a cooperative arrangement when Jesse was just approaching six, official first grade age.    This was not necessary as Pennsylvania's compulsory school age is eight, and I don't recommend this now to others unless you clearly know you have an exceptionally cooperative school district, as we did.

One of my important priorities was NOT submitting to standardized testing as an evaluation measure.  Along with a written description of our educational approach in all subject areas, I included a proposal for evaluation -- basically that we would share with the district a portfolio and written description of Jesse's on-going work and activities.

I was taken aback when my superintendent's first question was about "participating" in the district's standardized testing program.  I countered that I felt test results would not be necessary or useful to me as a parent/teacher, that I didn't feel these tests were accurate or helpful.  He AGREED with me, and said he wouldn't INSIST we take the tests, but encouraged us to do so for two reasons.

1. We might at some point want to put our son in school, and the test scores could be used to show proper "placement."

2. Even though he realized results from these tests weren't all that accurate, just taking them on a yearly basis would give my son practice in test-taking, so that if he ever did need to REALLY take one, he wouldn't be as anxious about the experience as he'd know what to expect.

He also made clear that test score results alone would in no way be used to decide if we would be allowed to continue home teaching.

I said the only way I could possibly agree to standardized testing would be if I were guaranteed that testing be done individually. I would not send my child into the regular classroom among 25 children he didn't know, with a strange teacher, in a strange setting. My superintendent immediately agreed to that, saying that would be no problem at all. I finally agreed, partly because, as my husband pointed out, it was their only request, and they were being so very cooperative about everything else. They made it very clear that they did not want to interfere in any way with our day to day work with our son. They trusted us.

Testing has been given by two different elementary school guidance counselors, who have both been very friendly and supportive. I made a point of going to the school with Jesse to look over the building and meet each guidance counselor well in advance of the actual testing. Jesse doesn't have an easy time in unfamiliar settings, and really needed this orientation time to feel comfortable. I didn't ask to be present at the testing, because I felt Molly and Jacob were too young to be left, and too young to quietly sit in the testing room with me. Jesse understood this. He also knew exactly where we'd be in the building during testing, and was with us during breaks. One guidance counselor even suggested we all go outside and play on the school swings for a bit in between test sections, and the kids all enjoyed having a whole playground to themselves!

Jesse has felt confident and good about the testing situation so far, something I'm much more concerned about than his "RESULTS," (which are, by the way, fine).

I do also give the district much more information about our on-going work than the bare numbers and percentages of the test score print-outs. I meet with the assistant superintendent twice a year to share what we've been up to. I literally bring a big box of stuff -- Jesse's records of books read, samples from collections, geodesic structures built, pictures drawn, lists of places where we've taken "field trips," samples of Jesse's writing, copies of magazines we subscribe to and use. I bring anything and everything I can think of that will help give a graphic, concrete picture of what we've been involved with. I'm also ready to describe specific learning situations -- how we once watched for an hour as a snake climbed up a huge maple tree in our woods, then read several books about snakes that night to find out what type it was, how then Jesse took two days to write up the experience, and how his story was later published in *Jibber Jabber*, a delightful children's newspaper put out by homeschooler Laura Duncan. In short, I'm not going to let test scores be the only way the district has of viewing our homeschooling.

Interesting, too, that although part of our initial agreement was that I would meet with the district twice a year to discuss progress, the district has NEVER called me to set up one of these meetings, and probably never would have or will. I call them; I set the appointment. I know some parents who initially agree either to meet with school officials who never call, or to file reports that are never asked for. So no meetings occur; no reports are filed. Tests usually aren't forgotten by school districts, though, and if you leave a district with test scores as their only means to judge what you're doing, it could backfire on you. I guess I also prefer going in on MY initiative rather than being "ordered" in. Maybe the old idea that the best defense is a good offense. I don't want any bad surprises or misunderstandings for any of us.

Here's another thing you may want to keep in mind when setting up arrangements for standardized testing with your school districts (a thing that most, but not all, Pennsylvania school districts require). Does your child usually read out loud or silently? This hit home for me when Jesse was close to 7, and considered an end-of-year first grader. We had scheduled his achievement testing with the very nice guidance counselor at the local elementary school, having no problems setting up individualized testing.

Jessie Schaeffer, a good homeschooling friend who is in our school district, was having a hard time working out the same arrangement for her daughter, Sunny, also 6 1/2. The guidance counselor at Sunny's respective elementary school claimed he certainly didn't have the time to give only one child a test, and that anyhow these tests were DESIGNED as group tests and therefore should ONLY be given in a group setting. Sunny had already had one bad experience going into a strange group of kids for "school ability" testing earlier that year, and Jessie didn't want a repeat. So she called me up, suggesting that perhaps Sunny, already a friend of my son, could take her test with Jesse. I readily agreed, thinking it could be a friendly experience for them, and make the testing situation a bit less boring. It seemed a great idea.

HOWEVER, in the middle of the night, I suddenly sat bolt upright; the problem with our new testing plan suddenly apparent to me. JESSE COULD ONLY READ ORALLY. This would make no particular difference in an individual testing situation, but reading aloud would certainly be considered highly distracting, if not outright CHEATING, when other kids were present. At home, it had felt very natural for Jesse to read aloud, as he was usually reading TO me or Jacob. He seemed to need the reality of actually hearing his voice out loud to be able to feel he was really reading. It was another half-year before Jesse began to really enjoy and see the point of silent reading, and do it a lot on his own. I knew I certainly couldn't expect him to make that sort of switch just for a test, and just in 2 weeks.

I called Jessie Schaeffer back the next day, and explained why we couldn't go through with the joint testing plan. She immediately said, "Oh, my goodness! I never thought of that! Sunny only reads aloud too!" Jessie finally worked out an individual plan for Sunny, and all went fine. This incident also made me wonder if some school children may be forced to read silently before they've had their needed time as oral readers. Maybe testing situations and "discipline" codes requiring silence are especially rough on beginning readers in schools. Anyway, it's certainly something to keep in mind when trying to figure out the best testing situation for your child.

## Keeping Records

Keeping homeschooling records -- do you or don't you? Some parents can't be bothered -- any form of record keeping seems a burden, artificial, not really communicating what is most important about their homeschooling experiences. I've felt that way myself at times. It seems to take too long; it doesn't seem useful. But I've changed my thinking about it, and I'm going to try here to inspire you to think more about why keeping some sort of records can be of help to you in teaching your kids, share some of what I've heard from others about the types of records they've found useful and easy to keep, and what has worked best for me.

One reality is that it protects US and our children if we keep honest records of their work and thinking and projects and interests and skills. If your child doesn't test well, or if you don't give your child tests, records can be "proof" that education is indeed taking place. For many, keeping regular records is already a requirement for homeschooling. Most homeschoolers who have been able to work out decent agreements with their local superintendents in Pennsylvania are required to keep some sort of records, or turn in some sort of regular evaluations of progress. Some districts want no more than a standard report card with letter grades filled in dutifully.

I was glad that my own district came up with an anecdotal

reporting form -- they really ask for what activities my children have been involved in, what their strengths and weaknesses are, etc. I'm sure my district would be very satisfied with a very brief summary, but I make it a point to spin these evaluations out -- I include just as much as I possibly can. I want my district to really understand that our kids ARE getting a wide, far-reaching, quality education. I tell about every fieldtrip, every social event for homeschoolers we've attended. I list all books read. I describe actual science experiments and questions the kids have raised about history and social studies. I describe their music, art and physical education activities. And I find that although this certainly takes some time to complete every nine weeks, it is a useful summary for ME to have. Really helps me and the kids take stock of where we are and what we've accomplished and where we may be missing out. When I have one of these evaluations filled out, I have no nagging sense that we might not be "doing" anything -- the sheer volume of it impresses ME as well as the school district. Why, I even admit to taking our last years' final evaluation report in to McDonalds and getting all the kids free cheeseburgers for all their many areas of "excellent progress." (No questions asked by McDonalds, either!)

At least one district now has it in their policy that parents must keep a daily log of educational activities, and make that log available for perusal. Unfortunately, they also specified the exact format of the record keeping, and some parents would probably feel uncomfortable with it.

Then there are the families who are quietly homeschooling without letting the district know about it. They usually realize they'd better have excellent records on hand if the "home/school visitor" (alias truant officer) quietly knocks on the door someday (it happens...). And many families who have children under the age of eight (compulsory school age in PA) are beginning to realize that keeping good records of activities and learning will help their case if they need to meet with school people eventually. This can be especially useful if the parent does NOT have obvious credentials to show. (Obvious progress by their child up to age 8 will show that they HAVE already been teaching very competently.)    Ruth Newell shared at the Homeschooling Weekend this past summer that knowing that she had a whole stack of notebooks filled with detailed descriptions of all their homeschooling activities for the last five years gave her plenty of confidence when she had to go in to meet with their district. She brought them all to the meeting, and could point to them and clearly let the school folks know that she was serious and conscientious. She was approved as a "private tutor" under Pennsylvania law with no problem.

Then there are the other reasons to keep records. They can help us feel more sure of what we're doing, let us realize more clearly that lots IS happening. I know that whenever I used to get in a rut of NOT writing in my various journals for a month or more at a time, thinking that I would SURELY just remember it all, those would always be the times when anxiety about not doing "enough" would surface. I would forget all the many things we might have accomplished -- all the questions, the experiments, the books we read, places we went, talking and discussing -- and look back in my blank journal and think that maybe we (sinking feeling) really hadn't DONE anything at all worth doing. Whenever, as right now, I'm in a good routine of writing in a journal/planbook daily, in fact all throughout the day, then I feel on top of things, more confident, more organized. And I think the kids respond to this too, and are more productive and organized themselves. I often tell them what I'm writing in my notebook about their accomplishments, and they are always pleased to know I'm keeping track of good things. It's a sort of memory book for us, a way of not forgetting good moments.

I think a lot of my initial difficulties with record keeping were that I hadn't yet found a format for record keeping that I liked. I scorned commercial planning books for a good while, and instead stapled together little booklets from scrap paper that I get from print shops. At one point I made a new booklet every month, and had each page labeled with the date (Jesse would help do this). I could stash the booklets in my purse, carry them with me anywhere, and I did write in them -- occasionally. But only pretty occasionally. I'd misplace them, forget about them, let many pages go by blank.

I tried organizing my booklets differently -- made little sections with subject headings, and tried to write several months worth of notes in one booklet. That didn't do it for me either. The booklets would get dog-eared and crumpled, they just didn't seem "official" enough to care about. The kids would scribble in them, I'd forget to write in them.

In a binge of "getting organized" I bought a standard teacher's plan book at the local office supply store and dug in. I of course used the little blocks for recording what we did, rather than for writing plans (I didn't plan much in those days... in any area). I used it a bit. A little bit. But it always felt so stifling, and so much was just left blank. Double page spreads of all those little blocks, with only two (maybe) filled in. And I had nowhere to jot little notes to myself, make lists, put addresses, ideas, brainstorms. There were just those little blocks, page after page. I dropped it, too.

I tried spiral notebooks, more homemade books, and was finally in another funk of not writing down much of anything, when I suddenly found the planning book for me (don't get me wrong, it might not do it for you, but it found me at the right time...). I was at the Lancaster Home Education Curriculum Fair last spring and one of the teacher stores represented there had a plastic-comb bound PLAN-IT FOR TEACHERS -- A COMPREHENSIVE PLANNING TOOL, designed by a teacher, Richard Glaubman.[9] I've heard that it's commonly available in most teacher stores. Runs about $7.00. I was home! This hand-lettered book felt comfortable to me, and useful -- AND I USE IT!!! I use it not only for keeping pretty detailed records of what we all do, but I use it for all sorts of planning and list making too. There are extras that weren't found in my other teacher plan

---

[9]Available from American Teaching Aids, Covina, CA 91722.

book -- full page calendars I can fill in for each month (good place to see at a glance what trips and outings we've had), an overview of each month (with space for making LISTS of priorities for each week), pages for setting daily goals, sections for listing appointments, phone calls to make, and then a nice friendly page after each week's little "boxes" where you're invited to put down "notes about students," "problems, concerns, opportunities, and successes," "goals needing more attention," and "spin-off ideas." I actually use all these sections, finding it wonderful to have a place to jot down everything now. I even made the book more useful to me by buying a 3-hole punch, and punching holes in all the pages of the book so I could put it all into a ring-binder (I personally don't get along well with plastic comb binding -- pages begin ripping out on about day three...) Now I can add things in as I want, put in oaktag pockets to hold "memorabilia" and extra information, slip our piano practice charts in the back, etc.. I even PLAN more now what I want to especially remember to do with the kids -- and I find that HELPS us, it doesn't stifle us.

Now maybe all this new organizational and record keeping ability is a direct off-shoot of having four kids -- the more kids you have the harder it is to keep everything effectively on mental file (although come to think of it, I was not very good at that with only one...). It really begins hitting home that being organized is the only way of coping at all. Or maybe it's because my kids are getting older and it seems more necessary and more natural to be more organized about all aspects of our homeschooling. I can't say. But personally I'm hooked on record keeping now, and don't think I could do without it.

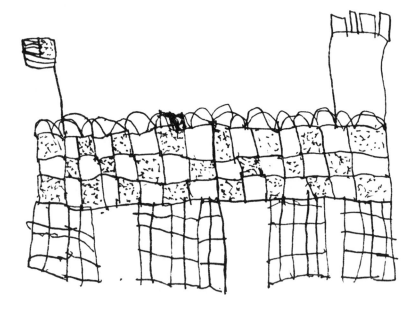

# 10. Writing Our Own Curriculum

Schools generally have carefully planned courses of study that carefully avoid teaching things over and over again. If dinosaurs are studied in first grade, then they won't be taught again in second grade, long division won't be introduced before simple division, and so on. Schools need to make careful plans so that the many teachers can work together. These careful, orderly plans are the school's "curriculum." Parents who teach their own children don't share the same difficulty. They know what their children know and what they have already done (unless of course the children had attended school for awhile!). While many homeschoolers use a correspondence school or "package" curriculum which sets out just such an orderly course of study, others, like us, follow their interests and their children's interests and flexibly build a curriculum as they go along.

Flexibility is the key word for what we write when we put our curriculum in print. We don't know exactly what we will be doing in six months, so, when we describe our curriculum to outsiders we tell where we have been. When Jesse was just six, Susan wrote about the pleasures of letting "serendipity" enter into the curriculum.

## On Serendipity and Homeschooling

"Serendipity" has long been one of my favorite words. I first came upon it by accident, appropriately enough -- I had discovered a wonderful tiny store in New York City named "Serendipity," and I loved their odd collection of this and that. It was some time before I learned what the store's name meant -- finding something by happy accident. What a delightful idea!

But the relationship between serendipity and homeschooling? It's just this -- I am being continually amazed how "happy accidents" keep opening and broadening our learning, indeed I now have to say that serendipity is our major mode of "curriculum design."

A few examples may show best what I mean...

First -- While looking through a bunch of old issues (second hand of course -- one of my healthy addictions is second hand books...) of *Cricket* magazine, trying to find an article I'd remembered about growing salt crystals (never found that...), what should I chance upon? *Part I* of a story about the four French boys and their dog who discovered Lascaux Cave in France. Our family had just visited Laurel Caverns *the day before*, and we'd been big into remembering all the cave references and stories we could. Jesse had asked me to retell the story of the four boys and their dog (we'd come across it in an archeology book sometime awhile back). I didn't know many details of the story at all, but did the best I could. So, serendipity came along the next day and brought us a detailed version, even if incomplete, as we were missing the issues with *Part II* and *Part III*. A week later, I was at a favorite Pittsburgh second hand book store and discovered in the last minutes of scanning the shelves a wonderful children's book on caves. It was just right for Jesse and me -- the adult book on caves and caving on our "grown-up" bookshelf was way over my head, too detailed, too much assuming a basic knowledge and vocabulary that I just didn't have. Then, a month later, we were at another second hand book store (found by accident of course, while looking for a clothing store...) and there they were -- the two missing *Cricket* magazines we needed to complete the Lascaux story!  We were thrilled!

Second -- In July, my boys bought a set of six miniature tractors with pooled birthday money.  One turned out to be a model *steam* tractor.  We'd *just found out* that such tractors existed from a birthday book, and were quite excited by the idea as my boys are both steam train "afficionados."  So, as we were driving away from the store on a back country road to visit friends, what do we come upon but a *real* old steam tractor!  We stopped the car, got out and looked it over -- it was just like the toy model!  We inspected boiler, firebox, toothed gears, power take-off, metal rimmed wheels, roof.  Then (was it even two weeks later?) we attended the Annual Steam Engine Exhibition in Portersville, PA.  (A family in our homeschooling network, out of the blue, had mentioned it to me, I'd never heard of it before...)  There was that same tractor again, along with many others, and four delighted and amazed Richmans.  (Molly wasn't born until the next night!)

Third -- After reading aloud the very powerful Newberry Award novel *Julie of the Wolves* by Jean George -- the story of an Eskimo girl lost in the Alaskan tundra and adopted by a wolf pack -- we decided to check out the Carnegie Museum's small Eskimo exhibit.  We'd never paid much attention to the display before, but now it was incredibly exciting to see a "ulu" or woman's knife just like the one Julie had treasured, meaningful to see Eskimo carvings on bits of bone and tusk.  As we left the museum, I was telling a museum shop clerk how excited we were to see the Eskimo exhibit that day, only to find out that -- you guessed it -- the museum was *just about* to open a whole new very large Eskimo section, with full size walk-in snow house, Kyaks, parka clad figures, everything...

Now, if I'd been a teacher in a school, it would have probably been considered poor planning indeed to not make sure I had appropriate reference materials and "activities" (translate: ditto sheets...) available *in advance* for planned "units" of work.  Look at all the proliferation of "complete kits" to teach everything in school -- preplanned schemes and progressions and levels for everything. How different and more delightful is our serendipity-organized life! We never know quite what we'll find, but we're gaining more and more trust that just speaking our questions will begin bringing answers and resources we'd never imagined. It really seems quite amazing that when once the questions are *raised*, our interest sparked, our eyes opened in a new way, that answers begin simply pouring in from every conceivable direction. Maybe it has to do with a readiness to see and take notice -- not readiness as defined in school ideas of, say, reading readiness, but rather an inner eagerness to perceive and fit certain pieces together.

Maybe this all points to one of the major problems of most schools -- there only the *teachers* get to ask questions, the students are only supposed to supply quick and correct answers. It's a rather lop-sided and unfair interrogation process. Instead of the true adventure, full of wonderful "happy accidents," that we're finding learning to be.

## Writing a Curriculum

If you need to seek approval for homeschooling from your school district, be prepared to do a good bit of writing. You'll most likely be asked for a "curriculum outline" or "planned course of study" for your children, which basically just means your overall plans and goals and possible resources you'll use in every subject area. It does NOT mean they want you to detail every moment of the next 180 days you spend with your child. It also does NOT mean that you have to PURCHASE a curriculum, though if you do, this of course makes your communication job much easier. You may then merely share with the district what you've bought, and it will in all likelihood look very official and get you approval. You can write up your own plans, though, and that is what this chapter is mainly about. And although the job can seem overwhelming at first, it can indeed be valuable to you in really sorting out your ideas, helping you realize what a good environment you are providing for your children at home. Here are some thoughts and ideas on how you might go about this work.

First of all, it means you will say SOMETHING about all of the required subject areas. In Pennsylvania, for example, for elementary school education, you need to say something about English (to include spelling, reading and writing); arithmetic; science; social studies (geography, history of the United States and PA, civics); safety education; health & physiology; physical education; music; and art.

THERE IS NO OFFICIAL "STATE CURRICULUM" OTHER THAN JUST SUCH A LIST OF SUBJECT AREAS -- it is up to each district to interpret these areas as they see fit. And so it should be up to YOU also to interpret them as YOU see fit. BUT say something about each subject. Don't leave anything out or you're setting yourself up for them to say your program is incomplete or not well-rounded.

To this I'd add another, purely optional heading -- social education of your child. Say something positive about your child's social opportunities -- family values orientation, sibling relationships, "peer" experience in outside classes or clubs, participation in any organized homeschooling events (fairs, potluck suppers, homeschooling weekend, field trips), family visits, service work in community, "team" participation, access to wide age range of friends, church activities, evidence of social responsibility, etc. Many school districts will hit you with questions about this -- be ready to answer with specifics.

Do feel free to stress that your program is INTERDISCIPLINARY, meaning that although you have written each subject up separately, that in reality, you try to INTEGRATE as many subjects areas as possible. (This just means do several things at once -- i.e. study fractions while doubling a recipe or learning musical note values, or use mathematics to help set up a history time-line or measure wood for a building project.)

Also it would be very appropriate to say something about your child -- his learning style, interests, hobbies, strengths, developmental "weaknesses" if any. Don't be afraid of making your child seem not quite perfect in every area -- Kathy Terleski found that her district really appreciated her honesty and insight in problem areas. You can use your description of your child in defending your particular plans, saying that you have tailor-made your curriculum to fit his/her special needs.

If your child has never been in school, you might want to describe what you HAVE ALREADY done, and then indicate that you plan to continue in the same way this upcoming school year. Use any good past successes as further proof of your qualifications to teach.

### List Resources

Make LISTS of everything that could possibly be listed that might have an impact on what you do with your kids. Later organize it all into subject areas where possible. You may decide not to actually include everything in your final write-up, but you'll feel better about having some "extra evidence" to pull out if needed.

Count books and periodicals in your home, perhaps in each subject area. Mention if you frequently go to bookstores with your child, or the library, or library book sales, or swap books with other homeschooling families, or give books as gifts to your children. Let them know you are LITERATE -- they won't necessarily assume you are. Unfortunately in dealing with most school people, you will have to prove your worth every step of the way. They may already have a mental image of homeschoolers as "abusive," totally uneducated parents, who can barely read or write, until you prove yourself otherwise.

List any "resource materials" you own or have borrowed from libraries -- tapes, records, films, videos, games, posters, science equipment (telescope, microscope, magnifying glasses, measuring cups, rulers, thermometer, etc.), globes and maps, sports equipment, art supplies, musical instruments. Don't worry too much if your child has not yet used these materials -- say you PLAN to use them, and list that they are available, that you always seek to provide your child with a wide variety of resources in all subject areas.

List any TRIPS you've taken in the past year, or plan to take in the coming year, and how you will INTEGRATE these into your "program" (make book about, scrap book, do experiments or art work as follow-up, tie in with history study, part of music appreciation program). Think not only of museums, and other "official" trips, but also of informal visits to friends' homes where your children might have been exposed to new ideas or "educational" toys or art or music, or to a new environment such as a farm, home-made house, or home business. Think of discussion ideas these visits generated, and list THEM.

List any family hobbies -- gardening (there's biology for you), cooking (math, chemistry, history, safety), pets (biology, responsibility, math -- how much does it cost to feed a goldfish for a year?), hiking (nature study, phys. ed.), going to concerts (music appreciation, social ability), stamp collecting (history, civics, art appreciation).

List any official textbook materials that you own, stating clearly that you purchased these materials yourself (this often impresses). Also list any "teacher"-type resource books you own or have read. Let them know that YOU know you can find the books you need to help plan a good program. After all, the textbooks that teachers use in college are not locked up in colleges -- they are often in your local library, second hand book store or library sale.

List any RESOURCE PEOPLE you are involved with, however sporadically. Good titles to use for these people might be "educational consultant," "curriculum advisor," "(specific subject area) specialist," or "private tutor," where appropriate. Think of librarians, private instructors, friends who happen to be certified teachers, friends who are enthusiastic about their fields or hobbies whom your kids might come in contact with (builders, friends from different countries, collectors, craftspeople, piano tuners, plumbers, etc.).

### Put a Coat and Tie on it

TYPE TYPE TYPE your final draft of your plan -- even if you have to barter services to get someone else to do it. Any format that makes your plan look more FORMAL, WELL-THOUGHT OUT, and ACADEMIC is useful with a tough district. You indeed want them to feel that you have gone to a lot of trouble to come up with your plan, and that you want it treated with respect. Typing is sort of like having your plan wear a coat and tie. Also keep in mind that the school people may not even read your document AT ALL, but they will look at its format and general headings.

Your philosophy and purpose CAN BE to have your children involved in choosing and planning and evaluating their own specific work, with your "parental guidance" of course. Don't feel you necessarily have to spell out EXACTLY what you plan to do in each area -- what specific books you'll read, etc.. You could instead state that your child will help in choosing and discussing books from a wide variety of types -- fiction, non-fiction, biography, historical fiction, mystery, folk-tales, drama, science, etc. Again, a goal you could write into your plan is that you want your child to realize the wide variety of books and resources available in all subject areas -- AND that is WHY you do not want to be limited to one textbook (such as the school district's). Just DON'T let the school people get the impression that you "don't do anything," just because you are not following some "canned curriculum" (or using their textbooks).

Do feel free to dress up your language a bit to make it seem more "educationese," but don't get caught in the trap of not knowing what you're saying (just like the school people...). Simple, clear writing is always good -- and appreciated. Here are a few terms that might be useful to you, though:

- *Sustained Silent Reading* (SSR) -- this just means that the child will choose his own reading matter, and read on his own without interruption or questioning -- you know, he'll READ. You might put in some time-frame on it -- "Jesse will be involved in a SSR reading program for at least 30 minutes daily, and keep his own record of books completed." SSR is a code word all administrators will know.

- *Sustained Silent Writing* (SSW) -- Yep, this is just plain old writing -- but writing that is self-chosen, not criticized by teacher while kid is writing. You might list here the types of writing your child has done, or that you hope to lead him to -- letters to friends or businesses, poems, journals, essays, submissions to magazines that publish children's work, reports on research, etc.

## Specify Evaluation Measures

Provide for some means of evaluation -- especially if you want to argue out of the yearly standardized test routine (not easy). Offer something ELSE -- you will share yearly a portfolio of your child's work in all subject areas, you will write up progress statements quarterly describing your child's work in all areas, you will have a private evaluator do a regular evaluation of your program, etc.. If you feel a strong point of your program is your history or science work, you may find that many standardized test do not measure ANYTHING about those areas. You may want to offer some extra documentation to the district about these areas if that's the case. In fact, do ask WHAT areas are tested yearly, what test they use, what the purpose of the testing program is (they usually have to say it is "diagnostic," that it is designed to help the teachers know strengths and weaknesses so they can teach better -- NOT so that they can "flunk" kids, OR so they can say you can no longer homeschool...). Even if you do agree to yearly testing, I'd still recommend you also try to meet regularly with school people to share concretely what you're doing -- you don't want them to ONLY have test scores to evaluate your child by, especially if your child doesn't happen to test well.

Ask to see the school's textbooks (teacher's copies if possible) and their curriculum write-up to "help" you in writing up your own plan. You can often borrow general goal and philosophy statements from these books -- and how can they refute them? Many of the schools' goals are fine -- for example, "All children will receive reading instruction based on their individual needs and appropriate to their potential for learning. It is essential every child develop a positive self-concept recognizing their unique abilities, but simultaneously an understanding of their weaknesses..."

In general, you don't have to change the way you're teaching in order to write up your own curriculum. You just have to learn how to put what you are already doing in the best light.

## Jesse's Fourth Grade Curriculum

When faced with writing an "official" educational plan this past year for Jesse, age 9 and considered by the district a 4th grader, I realized I had to come up with a touch (at least) of fancy language to describe what we do about reading. I knew I couldn't just say, "Oh, we just let Jesse read whatever he wants to and he reads a lot." So here is the admittedly somewhat overblown prose I finally chose. Mind you, it's not the way I'd talk about our reading at home to friends, but it seemed appropriate for the school folks, and apparently did the trick. They asked no questions.

Jesse will be involved in a literature based, sustained silent reading program, reading daily from self-chosen material for at least 45 minutes. He will try reading from many different genres: fiction, biography, plays, non-fiction in all subject areas, poetry, magazines, newspapers, etc. Length of readings will vary from short articles and selections to long childrens' novels (ie. *Caddie Woodlawn*, and other Newberry Award Winner books). He will keep his own record of books completed, and will discuss his reading daily with parent tutor. Attention will be given to noting the author's voice, appreciating style differences among different authors, comparing and contrasting similar books. He will focus on an author of choice and read several works by that author, comparing how the works are similar or different, how the author changed his approach or developed a consistent style. We will discuss tone, plot structure, characterization, recurring themes, use of language, and our own reactions and responses to the piece read.

We will not use a basal reader textbook, as our program is literature-based, and our goal is to allow Jesse access to the finest in children's literature and let him find his own reading level. We own at least 1200 children's books in our home, in all subject areas and levels of difficulty, and also use books borrowed from various libraries and homeschooling friends. We find that owning our own books gives a great love of reading, a sense of ownership of the whole process of reading, and we give great priority to buying books as gifts for the children.

Communicating with a school district is not the time to be as concise as possible -- if you can string something out, do so. (This may remind you a bit of the "padding" you may have done with term papers as a high school or college student. After all, in a sense you are dealing here with the same people once again.) But at the same time, do know what you are talking about and don't close yourself into corners of verbiage. Where ever possible give yourself options, outlets, other choices. I liked it that I did not lock us into saying we would read any specific books (an impossible thing for us to plan in advance), and I did not commit us to using ANY workbook or textbook type materials -- no comprehension drills, no vocabulary drills, no "five questions at the end of the story" stuff. Just committed us to real reading and talking about what we read. Just what we do best around here.

Some parents we've talked with wonder if they can feel confident in putting down in a plan or curriculum or evaluation that they just TALK about books and ideas with their kids. This on-going discussion with our kids, this conversation, may seem so natural to us perhaps that it doesn't seem important or worth mentioning, doesn't seem as concrete as saying our child has completed so many workbook pages or so many "skill" worksheets. But when we really start looking at what the real EXPERTS in the reading and language field say, I think we can gain more confidence in our folksy home approaches. After all, the schools would love to have as much discussion time as we have at home throughout our days -- they just don't have the time. I remember very well when I was a teacher in schools that it became a distraction if kids wanted to jump in with a comment about a book I was reading aloud to a group. It was a tangent that got us off track, and would soon have 20 other kids jumping in with their thoughts and reminiscences and anecdotes. But at home how different -- with just a few "students" we can explore all these tangents and let them become new roads to related learning. School teachers might love to be able to have book discussions during lunch time with their students (a common occurrence around here), but school cafeterias just aren't conducive to it.

We should feel confident and comfortable emphasizing the entire "literate environment" of our homes. Just look at what noted expert in the field Morton Botel wrote in the 1979 Pennsylvania *Comprehensive Reading/ Communication Arts Plan*, published by the Pennsylvania Department of Education itself:

> Before school and systematic instruction begin, the earliest means by which young children learn to read are by listening and responding to literature at home. In fact, a literate environment at home usually produces children who read early and maintain their competence throughout school. Such an environment has several characteristics. Family members have a general commitment to the benefits and pleasures of oral and written language. There is a home library and writing materials. Family members read silently, read aloud to their children and to one another, and talk about what they read with each other....
>
> The school should also provide a literate environment rich in language experiences that excite and challenge thinking and imagination, touch values and feelings, and improve reading and writing competence. For these purposes nothing is more effective than being exposed to literature by hearing and reading it and responding to its ideas, images and sounds.[15]

He continues to lambast (gently!) the schools for overusing "quickie" types of questioning and testing methods, urging instead the types of discussion and involvement common at home in families that love to read:

> Research shows that elementary and secondary teachers seem to overuse questions that call for short answers rather than those that generate discussion and involvement. Unfortunately they seem to be encouraged in this biased emphasis by the suggestions in many teacher's guides of basal reading and literature programs. The effect of this is to discourage and dampen student interest and involvement and thereby to limit the flow and quality of thought....
>
> We propose a variety of productive activities to tap all the four comprehension perspectives....

- discussions

- compositions

- oral and choral readings and rereadings

- simulations (role-playing and informal dramatizations)

- question/answer formats

- retelling (including retelling by changing characters, actions, or setting)

- art and music interpretations[16]

So this expert, very well known and respected in the field of reading, is advocating just the sort of thing most homeschooling families do with reading already -- and if this is advocated from such an expert, then we should feel proud of what we do and very confident to relate such things on our plans.

Translating this concretely, around here we read aloud a lot ("oral reading and rereadings"), and we talk about what we read ("discussions"), each of us getting a chance to share responses and ideas and questions. When Jesse and Jacob spent many happy hours building a pretend "Borrower's set-up" while we were reading the wonderful Borrowers series of books (all about imagined little people who lives inside the walls of houses and who "borrow" all the little things WE lose all the time...), they were involved in both a "simulation" and an "art interpretation."

For months any little throw-away was quickly grabbed by the
boys and turned into a Borrower stool or chair, a Borrower bed.
A leftover spice can became a miniature stove, scraps of woods
were glued and nailed into tables and benches, crocheted doilies
became fancy tablecloths and rugs. This was of course all self-
chosen play to them, not an exercise in "comprehension" that I
had cleverly devised -- I just gave them the space and the
permission and let them know I was interested in their ideas.
When they got all excited about imagining what would happen if
the Borrower characters were living here, or trying to imagine
future possibilities for them, they were engaging in "retelling by
changing characters, actions, or setting."

Or what about when Jesse tells me during lunch about the
wonderful book he's just been reading, *The Witch of Blackbird
Pond*, a Newberry Award Winner about a young woman accused
falsely of being a witch in colonial Connecticut. He lets me
know how he feels about the actions of the characters -- many of
them clearly unfair or narrow minded to us. He's responding to
the book personally and figuring out what the book means to
him. And when I ask him to retell parts of the story to me (it has
been 12 years since I last read the book myself, and I'm fuzzy on
some parts), then he's retelling with a real purpose -- he's
communicating with me because I really want to know about the
book too. I'm not just quizzing him or trying to check up on his
"comprehension skills." We are all responding to the book and
it's ideas. Our "just talking" is really talk and discussion of the
highest sort, and it's even largely initiated by Jesse.

You might even list it as a goal in any curriculum plan you
need to write that your child will "initiate discussion about
responses to literature through devising his own questions and
retelling parts he was particularly moved by." What
homeschooling parent hasn't been interrupted while reading
aloud to answer a question a child has about the goings-on in the
story, or what parent hasn't used a car ride to sometimes talk
over favorite parts of books with their kids? Not in any
"official" way that marks off this talking as a "lesson," but just as

part of the conversation.  I remember Jesse coming out with, "Hey, Mom, wasn't it funny when Peter Pan fooled the pirates that time on Marooner's rock?" on a car ride maybe a month after finishing reading the book together.  Our discussions don't have to be planned in advance as our kids feel that books just naturally are a good topic of conversation.

# 11. Getting Organized

Time can be the main problem for home-schooling parents who are feeling stressed-out both because they are not spending enough quality time with their families, and also because they do not have enough time to themselves.

I am in favor of the twenty-five hour day! If we could just have one extra hour then maybe we could do all the things that we want to do. Another way to find time was tried by one of my college friends, Mike Jones. He experimented with himself to see how little sleep he could get along on. Every night he slept a little less than the night before. He got himself down to about four hours of sleep every night. I don't know about you, but I begin to fall apart if I get less than seven hours...

### Feeling Stressed-Out

I have gotten a number of letters from families this past year who really seemed to be feeling much more negative about their homeschooling than positive -- the balance was tipped down. Way down. And although we all need to feel comfortable talking about the difficult days as well as the good days of homeschooling, I think when too many bad days come our way it's time to seriously re-evaluate what we're doing, and try some real positive CHANGE.

For some families the answer to too many bad days may indeed be for the children to go to school -- after all, it's not compulsory that we teach our kids at home. For most of us the answer may mean just that we have to get ourselves out of a down time by making a real effort to interact more productively and happily with our kids, to begin enjoying them more, and to break out of a cycle of negativity.

For many of us we need to find ways to make time for OURSELVES. Maybe by getting up earlier than the kids (I can hear the groans, but if you're a morning person, it's wonderful), or staying up after they are in bed (you know, not falling asleep while reading that bedtime story to the kids, like I'm prone to...)

Sometimes, too, we need to be more patient with ourselves, realizing that all sorts of factors beyond our control -- like lousy weather -- can make for some difficult times. If we all start snapping at each other around here, it always does us good to notice what the weather is doing -- usually it's gray, muggy and humid, that sloggy feeling before a storm. When the weather brightens, so do we. Being aware of this helps us not get into the blame and guilt routine.

The following are some of the letters I've received over the past year from mothers who, for any number of reasons, have been having rough times with their homeschooling. I really respect these women for having the courage to write about these feelings. I know some people feel discouraged after only hearing of the "glowing" side of things, and feel they must hide any lousy feelings they might have. These women took the step to get it all out -- and at least one told me later that just the chance to write it all out was the first step in getting herself out of her low time. Anyway, here are some of the letters... And for those of you who may think that here at our home we never have doubts, bad scenes, too much pressure, times when all is lost, I've even included a journal entry from a VERY bad day of ours here (two years back, so it's not SO painful now, and I can view it at something of a distance!).

One mother writes:

My attitude towards doing "school work" has mellowed lately which is good I believe. Unfortunately it is a side effect of too much personal stress in my life. We still use the Calvert materials but I'm more relaxed about when the work gets done. Maybe it's like when the glow of the newborn wears off and changing diapers and keeping the wash up, etc., is, well, more like routine work. I get *Growing Without*

*Schooling*, but have only read the first couple of pages of #47 so I'm behind there. And here I am renewing with you but I haven't finished the last issue. I'm tired of homeschooling. My husband doesn't help out other than give me occasional words of support. My son doesn't want to go to school.... There's a homeschooling support group forming in the area that I have just learned about and have sent for info on. Some get-togethers with others in the area would probably do quite a bit of good for me...

Here's another:

We have been homeschooling since the beginning. Our kids are doing very well both academically and in every other way possible. I'm very happy to be homeschooling them and love them dearly and am very glad to have them here -- BUT in the past couple of years I find I'm having a harder and harder time coping emotionally with kids always here and no breaks for me -- unless I go out evenings which I do at the expense of our "family time"... Anyway, I feel that there's so much written in a general way about homeschooling and how to do it -- legal things, etc. -- but not much written about how the mother copes emotionally with kids ever present and stays sane and still has some sort of creative life of her own. We live in a very rural area and don't have many friends close. The homeschoolers we knew when we moved here from Illinois 5 years ago in large part have ended up putting their kids in school for various reasons and the few we know that are still homeschooling are mainly very interested in structuring the homeschooling fairly strictly, which is not what we're doing. We're very UNschooled a la John Holt's ideas...

And from another mother...

You asked about our homeschooling year... It is getting mixed reviews at the present. There are MANY plusses, the largest being the joy of seeing my son free to be his own person. His natural interests are so different from most 1st graders... BUT there are some drawbacks. I never even read articles on stress in the past because I thought I was incapable of building up stress, but last September I practically had a nervous breakdown in panic over symptoms which have turned out to be vaso-constriction -- a reduction in oxygen to the heart when under stress. On the list of helps is relaxation.

The force of my son's personality and the sheer quantity of (incessant) noise he generates is a constant assault on my senses and I find by the time the girls come home at 4:00, I have no cushion built up during the day, my nerves are in a raw state, and I feel physically horrible. Like so many situations, it feeds on itself, for as I become depressed and distracted, I tend not to follow through in disciplining him and he gets away with doing less and less (chores) and becomes more out of control and harder to handle, and I become more depressed. Of course, not every day is bad, but I am concerned about the toll it may be taking on my health, and about the effects of all this in its many facets on my son....

Another mother writes...

I'm doing Home Schooling with three children, ages 8, 7, and 5, and also have an almost 3 year old daughter. I have some problems and I wondered if you might have some advice or tips to help me. My biggest problem is lack of patience. I feel under stress most of the time: I feel busy beyond by capabilities: I can't take care of the house, the meals, the laundry, and most importantly, the kids, the way I would like. There is nothing I would rather do than spend my days with my kids. I don't understand my impatience, but I feel badly for the kids. (This sounds like a "Dear Abby" letter, but I'm just hoping you might have some tips that will help us.) We have chosen Home Schooling for Religious reasons and we use the Our Lady of Victory Home Study Program. I LOVE the course, and so do the kids....

And from a later letter from the same mother...

Thank you so much for your wonderful letter. It was a great help to me, especially when you said it was a concern of many parents (the stress, strained nerves, and impatience). I thought that I just wasn't cut out for Home Schooling. I've been told by people close to me that I'm too much of a perfectionist, I'm too organized, and I expect too much of my kids and myself. On top of all of that, I am very slow at what I do. I also have some outside of the home concerns with my mother that take me away too much. We have made a few changes this year that should help....

And now for MY story. Again, this is a journal entry from

several years ago, and I even tore it out of my notebook and stashed in the back of a desk drawer -- it's not easy to admit we have these times, even to ourselves...

This has been a painful time for Jesse and me, this trying to establish new homeschooling routines and expectations. It infuriates me at times when he seems so easily frustrated, so always close to tears, so resistant to suggestions. As Holt said, he's not letting ME be the "fine creative, motivating teacher" I like to see myself as. Visions instead of failing, failing miserably, making my son into a pressure cooker of anxieties, a short fuse bundle. Also frustrating that I am too exhausted to get up early in the morning, and our day starts at 10:30 and time slips by improperly used. No writing. No seeming memory of how he used to spell words (talking here of just REASONABLE spellings, not "correct"), leaving out all blends and ending consonants other than *s*, etc... Drives me wild to see him shift his weight in a chair, slouch down, wiggle, yawn, fiddle with his pencil, rearrange his paper -- WASTE TIME... Me -- always aware of our STEALING time, of not wanting to spend all DAY on this writing work. And Jesse then TAKES all day just to barely begin. I long for an end to vacation, for a full week of getting back to a reasonable schedule. Also drives me wild that Jesse seems often so enthusiastic on HEARING of a new idea, apparently eager to start (tomorrow!), and then it is cement feet time when tomorrow comes. Good to hear that Meg Johnson [used to publish a homeschooling paper] has also threatened hers with school if they can't find better ways of getting on -- the ultimate option. Then of course I curse myself for lack of patience, for putting such pressure, for exploding as I do, for doing just what I know will set HIM off -- seemingly BOTH of us just ready to pounce at the chance to do whatever we KNOW the other will HATE. Making us hate our time together...Intense learning time for us all now....

So, there you are folks, for those of you who have thought I only have positive dealings non-stop with my kids. I think the day I wrote this entry was the day that Jesse literally ran out of the house crying, saying he'd NEVER come back. All over a writing idea I was pushing on him (he was 7). We all do have times that leave us feeling wilted, dismayed, guilty, times we're not proud of.  I know one thing that has helped here is learning to apologize to the kids when I've really been out of line about something -- as they do with us.  And I always try to look at the whole day -- do we go to bed angry still?  I think I can say truthfully that we don't.  If we all blow up at times around here, we're also quick to recover and go on and make up and come at the problem from another more positive direction, or just find a different direction entirely and forget the lousy one.  I think we're gaining trust in ourselves by going through this sometimes painful process -- trust that we CAN find solutions.  We wouldn't know we had that in us without some kinks along the way.

I think the issues brought up by all these letters bear more looking into -- how CAN we manage to find time for ourselves in our day, how much interaction do we need with other homeschoolers to be able to maintain our enthusiasm for what we are doing (thinking about OUR social needs, not just the kids!), how do we communicate our needs to our kids in realistic and positive ways.  And perhaps most important, how do we stop over-loading our circuits with TOO MUCH (in my case, our bad scene took place very shortly after we'd moved to the big farm house on the property, and a move of any sort is a stressful time for anyone).  I'm reminded of those lists you see in articles on "Managing Stress" -- all the point values assigned to all the major life changes or problems that can build up to be just TOO MUCH, in this case the straw that can break the homeschooling mother's spirit.  Let's help each other ease the burden.

## Organizing the Homeschooling Day

Many parents have written asking for a concrete look into a typical homeschooling day -- how do families decide what to do and when?  How do they structure their time?  Is it even RIGHT to structure time?  Hope you can share what your family has worked out that works for YOU, and for starters here's a look into our home...

We began a new strategy last December, shortly after our move to our new house.  We finally had most boxes unpacked, and it seemed like time to get our days back on track. Piano, writing, and math work had all slid during the weeks and months of work on the house. Our energies had necessarily been focused on scraping, priming, painting, sanding, tear down and build up -- how welcome the thoughts of settling down instead to piano, writing, math and more reading! I realized then, too, that not only were all of us a bit rhythmless, but I was spending too much time on the phone during the day, mostly long, involved homeschooling calls. Time for a new direction and plan.

Discussing the issue with the kids, I proposed, first, that I would try earnestly to limit all phone calls to 5 minutes or less during the daytime. (So, friends -- call me after 5:00 p.m. Better phone rates for you, too!) The boys were grateful, and would literally run and set the kitchen timer for me when the phone would ring.

We then set about making a chart of the day -- a "time-line" showing all the hours from 8:00 to 4:00, the times Daddy wasn't home. We had to realize that when Howard was home the kids wanted to be with him, playing or helping with work about the place, rather than do anything else. Our time was different then, valuable of course, but changed. What we needed was to take full advantage of the earlier in the day time.

Jesse knows all about my *Side-Tracked Home Executives* file card system (often ignored for weeks on end, but still helpful), and so he knew what I was talking about when I asked him to think of all the daily homeschooling work he thought we should be doing. Then on to weekly or special projects. We wrote these all out on separate cards. Here's what we came up with for "Dailies":

- Do Some Math Work (with a dozen or more possible activities listed on card)

- Do Some Writing.

- Silent Reading time -- everyone choose a book, no phone calls.

- Piano Playing -- 30 minutes each.

- Recorder time -- 15 minutes.

- 10 minute Race (that is, turn on the radio to classical music, and race around our 'grand circle route' from living room to dining room to project room and around and around. Good for winter when we couldn't get outside as much).

- Exercise time (gymnastics, dancing, or physical fitness self-testing. Finding it's always good to balance out sitting down times with action -- banishes doldrums and fidgetiness).

Weeklies were "Special Art Projects," "Do a new Science Experiment," "Work on History Time-Line," "Do Wood-Working in Basement," etc.

Every weekday morning now, Jesse sets up the day by tacking his cards up on our "Day." He decides when we'll do each thing, and also what that specific activity will be. I offer suggestions at times, but the final decision is his. Takes about 5 minutes to get the "Day" going -- often if I'm really together I can get the breakfast dishes done while Jesse is deciding on his arrangement.

Now don't get us wrong -- we aren't able to accomplish everything we set out to do each day, and we don't clock ourselves to the minute or adhere slavishly to the day's plan. We've sometimes come up with a plan that's impossible to follow, or perhaps one project lasts a whole morning rather than the 30 minutes we thought it might. We learn from all of it. What this idea IS giving us is a new understanding of time and how we use it, and it's helping us focus our energies more positively. We find we accomplish much more than before and without my getting NAGGY. Instead of interrupting the boys' play with an unwanted directive, I can now usually just ask Jesse what's coming up next on his schedule. And if we need to change something, we do.

Some ideas that we'd TALKED about for over a year became realities. We finally stopped just talking about making a history time-line in our upstairs hallway, and instead scheduled it in and took the hour to DO it. Instead of my trying to urge Jesse to read silently at odd moments when I thought it would be a good idea (say, when I was busy sweeping), now we all sit down to a silent reading time together. Jesse's been writing daily again -- sometimes letters, sometimes entries in his homemade journal, sometimes little articles, sometimes a pretend newspaper, sometimes poems or riddles or signs. He decides. New cray-pas drawings and yarn stitchery pictures and wood scrap sculptures are on display.

During these months of experimenting with new ways of structuring our time, we've tossed out some cards, and made other new ones. We're realizing how to juggle our time a bit more effectively and creatively even on busy days of visiting or appointments or chores. Perhaps Jesse can do his silent reading while Jacob is in the dentist chair, or during a long car ride. Maybe we can run laps around our driveway while the goats are finishing up their feed in their milking stands. We're enjoying the variety of our days, and also enjoying the stability of regular time blocks. For us, right now, it seems to be the right balance, the right track...

### Getting Rid of the Big Time Waster

**Often people ask how Susan and I find so much time to do the many things that we do. Perhaps the most important factor is that we don't waste our time watching TV. About a year ago, Susan wrote in a letter to GWS...**

We have been TV-less totally since Jesse was a year old. A one week experiment of putting the TV in the closet just kept on and on, until finally Jesse took the whole thing apart last summer with screw driver and hammer, and saw what the insides were like. He even ended up salvaging the TV's speaker, and wired it up with leftover telephone company wire so he has a speaker from our stereo in his bedroom. (He has also wired me a speaker salvaged from an old tape recorder so I can have music in the kitchen... He does all this electrical work completely on his own, rewires lamps too.)

I think the lack of TV in our family has been a MAJOR factor in helping us raise children who are NOT consumer-toy oriented. We do not have neighbor children nearby that our kids see, so we don't have the problem some families do of finding their TV-less kids just go to the neighbors and watch and watch. Our kids have always been critical of other kids who watch TV all the time -- they really can't understand why someone would want to waste their time like that. They also have completely accepted it that we ARE a TV-less family, and I think take pride in the fact that we are different.

We certainly have not tried to hide our feelings about TV from the kids, and we do have a number of other friends, all homeschoolers, who have chosen not to have TV either. Of course, the kids do see a few shows a year, at someone else's home, usually a public TV nature show or maybe a ballet, and we always enjoy discussing the show for a long time afterwards, finding that we really get our mileage out of the few shows we see. A few shows a year is clearly enough for us.

I really like the book *The Plug-in Drug*, by Marie Winn where she makes the very important point that TV is not just an addictive "drug" for kids, but also for PARENTS -- it becomes such an easy babysitter, such an easy way to get the kids quiet and out of your hair. Just plug the kids in. They happily zombie out while you can get on with your adult life. But what a price!

I feel about the no TV question very much the way I feel about homeschooling itself. It's a choice that we do have the power to make within our own homes. Our choosing not to send our own kids to schools won't make schools go away, and our choosing not to have TV in our home won't make TV go away. And I'm not on a neo-Luddite campaign to smash TVs everywhere (or tear down schools). We've just tried it in our own family and have found that frankly we have SO MANY things that we LOVE to do with our limited time on this earth, that TV (and school) just can't be allowed in.

I remember when we first put away our TV, Howard kept saying to me, "But how could we have wasted so much time just WATCHING TV before? We have so much time now." We are often asked by homeschooling friends how we ever have the time to do as much as we do, and not having TV to eat up hours and hours a day is one very important help.

I also think that choosing to have, or not have, a TV in your home should be a very conscious decision, based on firm conviction. I know some families who flip back and forth twenty times on the TV issue -- one week it's TV with no restrictions, the next it's taboo and gone, next month it's cartoons all day. I wonder what messages these parents are sending their kids. I think it would certainly be better to accept TV and carefully monitor use so that it doesn't become addictive and overtake family life entirely, than to just keep jumping from side to side of the fence, giving the kids no firm base and guidance.

For us it was one of those eye-opening things to even realize that we could make a personal choice about TV. We could say yes, or we could say NO. Same thing with schooling. Our society might like us to think we can't make these choices, but we can. For us, it's been the right one.

## Scheduling Time for Dad With Kids

At the beginning of this chapter, Susan wrote about the way she organized the part of the day when I was not home. Not long after that we scheduled our evenings as well. I don't know what your memories of schedules are. Maybe you remember being in the middle of something when the bell interrupted. Maybe you think of a particular moment sitting in class, watching the clock, waiting for the bell to ring.

Well, schedules have all of those faults, but they also have one tremendous advantage: They give you a period each day when your time is your own with no one else making demands upon it.

Before we instituted our evening schedule, I would come home from work and would try to sit in "my" chair and unwind and read the newspaper -- and the family would descend upon me.

Susan's feeling was, "I have been with the kids all day and need a break. Now Howard can take the kids." She wanted to go up to our study and write articles for our newsletter. At about this time I read Nancy Wallace's book about her family's experience with home education, *Better Than School.* The reason that Nancy had enough time to write her book was because her husband would take her children at 3:00 each day for a couple of hours.

My feelings, as I would try to keep the family at bay, were a mixture of annoyance and guilt. I was annoyed that I could not have any time to relax without being the victim of assault, and guilty that I was short-changing Susan and the kids.

Jesse and Jacob and Molly's feelings as they pounced upon me were, "Let's see if Daddy will play with us now." They had discovered that the way to check if Daddy would play with them, was to just start playing with Daddy. Then if Daddy crouched into a shell or yelled in an unfriendly way, maybe he wasn't in the mood.

Saturdays and Sundays, my days off each week, were even worse. Whenever I would come in from farm work and try to read a book, the after-school scene would repeat itself. I had a problem -- no time to myself that I could count on. Susan had a problem -- no time to herself that she could count on. And the kids had a problem -- no time with Daddy that they could count on. Finally we all got together and discussed the problem and arrived at a schedule that satisfied all of us.

Our original schedule began when I would get home from work at about 3:30 after a day of teaching. I would have free time to relax or do whatever I wanted to do until about 5:30 when we would eat dinner. After dinner, Susan would wash the dishes, then we would all spend 15 minutes cleaning up the house. Then for an hour, Susan would go up to our study while I would play with the kids. My original playtime with the kids was divided into segments with each child having fifteen minutes to decide what he or she wanted to do, and then me getting fifteen minutes to choose what I wanted us to do. Sometimes the children choose rough and tumble games, sometimes more quiet activities. After their choices, I would usually choose to read to them.

The agreement has evolved over time. Our current "summer vacation" schedule calls for me to take the kids for two hours a day at 3:00, giving Susan a time to herself that she can count on. We also have a family clean-up-the-house time after supper. The rest of my time is basically mine to allocate how I wish. My two hours with the children are split between one hour when the kids decide what we do and one hour when I decide what we do. The kids look forward to their special time with me and they often plan in advance what they want to do during that time. Last summer, during my time to choose, we would cook supper over a campfire or read about the history, archaeology, and religion of Israel (*The Source* by James Michener). Molly (age 2) did not like listening to such adult books, so I usually would keep her busy while we read by getting her eating, swinging, or playing in the sandbox.

I am sometimes finding some of the children's playtime choices to be unenjoyable times to endure -- but at least such times only last at the most for about fifteen minutes. Other times I have found to be quite enjoyable, as when we played variants of chess all through many playtimes last winter.

I have always been a game-player. I have competed in chess tournaments and bridge tournaments and in general I am quite intrigued by games of strategy. As a child I remember fondly the many times when my sisters and I used to play bridge with our parents. I also remember that when friends would come over we would usually get out a deck of cards or a board game.

In many ways Susan and I are quite compatible, but not when it comes to playing games. Her childhood memories of playing games are not so pleasant. A few times I have dragged her into bridge games, but only with great difficulty.

Well, anyway, last winter we were all playing "variants" of chess during our play time. Molly, at age three, was into it more than anyone. You may wonder what I mean by "variants" of chess and you may wonder how a three year old learns to play chess. Let me go back to the beginning.

I taught Jesse, who is now nine, how to play chess when he was about four. I have hoped to develop game players in my family who I could play with. Jesse learned to play chess over a period of about two months. We started off very simply, with just pawns and kings and rooks, so that Jesse could learn to move those pieces without feeling overwhelmed. Jesse and I played a number of games with only those pieces. When he felt comfortable with the movement of those pieces, we gradually added queens, bishops and finally knights. Soon we were playing with the full complement.

One problem we had, at first, was that Jesse hated to have any of his pieces taken. I still think that there is something death-like about the loss of a piece and it is very difficult to lose them even for the short span of a single game, even if your opponent has lost many more pieces. Jesse and I eliminated this difficulty by frequently playing a chess variant called "jail" chess. The only difference between "jail" chess and regular chess is that when you take an opponent's piece in "jail" chess, you don't remove it from the board, rather, you put it back on an available empty square of your choice. Gradually, as Jesse became more comfortable with losing pieces, we graduated into playing more normal chess. Often I would handicap myself by taking off several of my pieces to make the game more equal. Jesse did not like losing and to keep him playing, I made sure that he seldom lost.

When Jacob, now six, was three, I taught him to play in about the same way I had taught Jesse. At first he simply joined in my "jail" chess games with Jesse. He moved the knights, which Jesse and I called "magic knights." Essentially he was allowed to move the knight anywhere he wished on the board.

One day, I started him, as Jesse, a few pieces at a time. He learned quickly, having been involved with those "jail" chess games. One of his favorite opponents was our monkey puppet. Monkey has long been a favorite part of our playtimes since Jacob was born, and is constantly doing outrageous things, much to Jacob's delight. Before Monkey begins playing, he always claims to be a "very tough" chess player and claims that he has "never lost" a game. Then during the game, he often tries to slip Jacob's pieces off the board or put his own pieces back. Somehow he is always caught. When Jacob finally wins, Monkey chases him around the house trying to get his king back. Once Jacob let Monkey win on purpose. Jacob doesn't mind the few times that Monkey wins, though he has trouble when Jesse or I beat him.

Until recently, Jesse and Jacob haven't played much chess with each other. I still remember the catastrophic game that they played when Jacob was three. Six year old Jesse had given himself a handicap: He started with just a king and one paun so that he surely wouldn't be able to win. Then sheepishly he proceeded to advance his paun down the board, turn it into a queen and win. Three year olds don't take losing well.

Now-a-days, Jesse as a mature nine year old seems to imitate me when he plays with Jacob -- he sort of lets Jacob win. I watched them play a game together last night. Jesse started with several fewer pieces then Jacob and proceeded to checkmate Jacob. Jacob, at six, stood looking at the chess board, biting his lower lip, then Jesse moved one of his pieces away from the checkmate. Jacob moved up his knight. Jesse pretended not to notice that his king was being attacked. Then Jacob took Jesse's king.

Molly, at three, is the quickest study of all. Before I

actually started to teach her how to play chess, she renamed all the pieces. The king was the "daddy," the bishops were "cookies," the rooks were "lollipops," the queen was the "mommy," and the pawns were "children." In about a week's time, she moved from playing with just kings and pawns to playing with the full complement. Molly enjoys jail chess, monkey chess, and all the other variants of chess. Our latest is monkey blindfold chess, where Monkey pretends to play blindfolded but really keeps peeking over the top of his blindfold.

I expected Molly to have the same trouble if her pieces were taken as Jesse had had as a three year old. I thought this would be intensified as she readily identified the pawns as children. This was not the case. Molly, being much more in tune with worldly affairs than the boys, has already asked us many questions about death. She has been aware when baby goat kids or kittens have died, and she has no trouble with the temporary removal from the board of plastic chess pawns. But chess for her is not all death and competition. This afternoon when I got home from work I found her in the livingroom playing with the chess pieces by herself; the black and white pawns were together on the edge of the board having a party.

So now you know some of the variations of chess that are going on in the Richman home and how I am engaged in my long term plan to develop more game players in the family. Let's see now, in about four years the three should be old enough for us to start playing bridge!

## Sibling's Special Time with Each Other

My special time with the kids inspired another special time -- Jacob's special time with Molly. When Jacob was six and Molly three, Susan wrote...

Jacob, my 6 year old middle child, now has a job. He makes about $1.00 a week at it, his pay-day being Friday afternoon. I'm his employer. His job? Babysitting for our 3 year old Molly while I have a concentrated 50 minute piano practice time with 9 year old Jesse. This new arrangement is working happily for all of us. Although Molly would sometimes understand about not bothering Jesse and me at the piano, and play happily nearby or look through books or draw, too often we'd have an unhappy (OK, miserable) scene where Molly would work herself into a rage trying to climb up in my lap, bang on the keys, knock our books off, etc. Also Jacob would sometimes seem to drift about during this time, often rather vacantly gazing off into space curled up in an arm chair. I'm of course not saying kids shouldn't have peaceful quiet times like this, but it was seeming to me that Jacob wasn't particularly gaining either. He would rarely play actively during Jesse's piano time, but seemed to just be in a suspended "waiting room" vagueness. And at times all of our exasperation levels were rising dangerously, and all my patience and Jesse's would be lost.

Jacob's new job is solving all these problems. Now in his third week of WORK, Jacob is even beginning to plan ahead his "special time" with Molly -- "Maybe tomorrow Molly and I could make up a pretend store," etc. Molly is getting familiar with the whole idea, and often runs over to grab Jacob's hand, ready to go off to HER special time with HIM. They've been building with blocks, dressing up in outrageous outfits, playing pretend games with dolls and stuffed toys, imagining all sorts of dramas. They've baked cookies and muffins together without any help from me (Jacob is our resident creative baker, his forte being carob EVERYTHING, no recipes needed and it almost always is edible...). They've laughed and giggled and been HAPPY now during this former wasted part of their day.

And Jacob is also happy about earning his own money. He's planning on buying a few small apple trees for our future orchard and has also purchased a small set of colored pencils and spends much time delightedly counting his money. (He hasn't needed any workbook pages or pretend money to learn about pennies, nickels, quarters and dollars -- he uses the real thing!) I know many, many families don't feel comfortable or right about paying their children for jobs around the home, and prefer giving kids an allowance so the kids can have some money. My boys have always been bewildered about the idea of allowances, and have never wanted one, and they DO do many jobs for NO pay (and fairly cheerfully). This job is an extra special job that I especially appreciate Jacob doing, and the pay (25 cents a time IF Molly doesn't come to bother us before the time is up) does seem to help Jacob take this work very seriously and proudly. And as for allowances, Jesse recently said he thought allowances were sort of like "Welfare for Kids" (we'd just been reading a kids' book on the history of the social welfare system in our country) -- and that he'd rather work for his money.

And, of course, Jesse and I are having much more productive piano times now that Molly is not trying her darnedest to "disturve" us. We know now we can count on a long stretch of concentrated time to work together, without feeling we're in the middle of a three ring circus. Might be something for some other homeschooling families to consider when dealing with several children at once.

One caution -- one of Howard's early memories from childhood was of a day when he was, for some reason, bugging his mother while she was doing some sort of work, and his mother, in exasperation, finally offered to pay his older sister Janice a dollar if she could just DO SOMETHING with Howard for a while and keep him out of her hair. Howard was terribly affronted, and felt that at least HE should have been paid too. He certainly didn't feel like cooperating with the scheme. I think Howard, at the time, was a good bit older than Molly -- she is not quite aware of money matters particularly, although she knows she IS Jacob's job. But for her, at this age, this just makes her feel special and important. Very important to work these things out positively, so that it doesn't feel like blackmail or trickery.

I can imagine this might also be a possible help to the mothers who've written that they feel overwhelmed and very stressed with NO free time to call their own, especially when their husband's work doesn't allow him time to take the kids for a spell. Perhaps the older CHILD could take the kids for a while if this were clearly proposed and discussed with them, and parameters set together...

## Moving Towards Positive Traditions

There's a big question that's always popping up when I open the day's homeschooling mail, or talk with families at a homeschooling gathering. It's this -- "But how STRUCTURED are you in your homeschooling???" It's a main question mothers are always asking each other, and we probably don't usually give very satisfactory answers. We may blithely (or embarrassedly) say, "Oh! we're not structured at all!," or conversely "Oh, we use the such-and-such curriculum and really have to have a tight schedule." What we all are probably hoping for, though, is a real inside look into another family's homeschooling. We'd love to see a "normal" day in someone else's home -- who decides when everyone gets up? Is the day a set routine, and if so, who set it up, and is everyone happy and cooperative about it, or snarling and fighting it the whole way? Do the kids on their own move from purposeful activity to activity, or is Mom trying continually to wheedle them into a "learning" activity? Does the mother at least need to be part of things in an active way, especially in transitions from one subject to another -- or are there really no subjects, but just real living and learning? What is the rhythm of the day, the ebb and flow? How "much" gets done -- and who decides if this is enough? How much regularity is there to the day? How much is each day unique? And is regularity boring or freeing?

I've come to feel that's it's impossible to really ever see what happens at another home -- when we visit we change the day's expectations entirely (and rightly so!), and we're not seeing the "normal" day. All the more reason why we need to write and talk and share with each other about what our day-to-day is really like (including the occasionally inevitable tantrum -- from child or parent!), as well as the good discoveries we've all made in learning to live with and guide our children.

Here's an update on our own lives:

I wrote earlier about the plan we began using just a year and a half ago to help organize our homeschooling day. (A new organizing idea seemed really necessary as we were in a transition time after making a house move.) It basically involves a card charting system that Jesse can use to plan his own use of time, within parameters I've helped him set. He has total say over WHEN certain types of activities will take place -- he can choose to have his piano time before lunch or just after breakfast, or whatever. But he can't choose not to play piano at all (this is certainly not to say that we don't "forget" at times in the delight of doing something else, but still this daily expectation keeps us on track). Jesse also helps choose just what it is that he'll actually DO in each area he sets up in his day, and I know that this freedom to decide makes him not balky about the whole plan. I seriously listen to any suggestion he has, however outlandish it may seem to me at first. I sometimes offer other suggestions, and we work out something we can both feel happy about. And my knowing that he has visualized that he will devote time in these areas keeps me from being naggy with him (cuts down on the "Now Jesse, when are you ever going to do your writing????"). Another important ingredient is flexibility, and our growing ability to balance out our active time and quiet time, and to know when to change the day's plan mid-stream.

Basically, we're still finding this way of planning incredibly helpful to us, we're still using it, in fact using it better now than last year. Now this article is not urging you to try our plan (I'd even go so far as to guarantee it WON'T work for you!). It's just what we've evolved over time, and every family has to do their own search for their own positive way to structure time with their children. Pasting on someone else's solution denies you the chance of finding something even better, something more suited to your unique family style. I do think, though, that we can all gain from hearing concretely why some things seem to go very well for certain families, and why some flop. Can point out possible directions we hadn't thought of yet ourselves.

I think, first, our "Setting up the Day" plan has been good for us because it's really become a TRADITION for us -- it's just what we expect to do in the morning. It's become embedded in our homeschooling now, Jesse pinning up his subject area/project cards on his time-line of the day, gathering focus and then starting in on the day's work. Jacob (5 1/2) has asked to have HIS own day now, and though he certainly doesn't use it as regularly as Jesse, it's there on the bulletin board in the dining room now, and will be there when he (and I) are REALLY ready to approach his day this way. By edging into this, he's slowly gaining ideas about planning and decision making. And he's following a tradition set by his brother.

I use the word "tradition" here purposely, as I think it's a key, and because I think possibly the idea of forging family traditions has a more positive ring to it than "getting structured." For some homeschooling families the very word "structure" is an incredibly negative word, bringing up images of drill sergeants and bells ringing to march students off to the next subject. It's a much maligned word, just like "discipline" (which carries images of frowning disapproval and spankings and children who just won't "mind"). For some it's downright embarrassing to admit to "structuring" their time -- I get letters from parents who apologize for not being "ready" to just turn the kids "loose," for not being "John Holtish" enough. They may forget that John Holt was a person who at times in his life made it a tradition to rise at 4:00 in the morning so that he could play cello for THREE HOURS before he would need to go to teach school. He was also fond of saying that there was NO situation that didn't have structure to it, that structure is just a part of life at all levels, from the cell or atom to the universe. Different structures allow different things, of course -- the structure of an amoeba allows it to do some things we can't do, but our more complex structure lets us do many other things. And so it is with our time, too. I remember being taken up short when I read recently that the great composer Bach once said that time was the one true gift of God -- it's the only thing he gives us just once.

So maybe in sorting out our ways of using time, TRADITIONS is something we can positively think about, and see how this idea -- that can work so well in many areas of our living with children -- may have some help to give us with our homeschooling. I think of the many and varied traditions that have cropped up in our family over the years, often beginning quite accidentally. It's now a tradition that the boys set our holiday dinner table in private, usually layering on several lacy tablecloths, climbing on step stools to secretly reach the fancy china, opening up the old silver chest to get out the inherited real silverware. And the kids all go off to the woods to help Howard tap maple trees in late winter (sweet smells of boiling syrup fill the house now as I write). And they get to open Christmas presents on Christmas MORNINGS, not the night before. And Jesse, and soon Jacob, gets to read the important "four questions" at our Passover Seder meals. All the little things that become repeated year after year, treasured and looked forward to, a beginning of a heritage.

On the day to day level, it's also a tradition that we all eat three meals together, and I know the kids feel incredibly adrift and unsettled and visibly unhappy if somehow, say, lunch gets skipped because we've just all snacked the day away. Jacob will moan, come 3:30, "but we never had lunch!" We seem to need these regular joining together times, times to regroup, and then move on to the next round of activities. The kids expect it. It's what we do. Also I think my kids would mutiny if our loved bedtime routine of nightly reading aloud up in their double-bed bunk were suddenly, and arbitrarily, done away with one night. If they got the feeling that this special time was only available by caprice or whim and not by firmly established, long standing tradition.   (Likewise I would mutiny if my two hour typing/writing time each day were arbitrarily done away with for too many days in a row, if I got the feeling that I couldn't count on having time alone to think and write... we've structured this into our day, too. We can't forget our own needs.)

We've also found it positive to purposely structure in many NEW traditions.  We now have a chart on the dining room wall relegating nightly table setting duties, and a regular system of deciding WHO gets to choose what we have for breakfast, and who will make it (ending -- almost -- the grumpy morning whines of "But I hate cream of wheat!  I want cheese eggs!") We also have a long list posted next to our upstairs bathroom sink telling us what we need to do before going to bed (I have to admit here that it was only after putting up this chart that I began being a regular "dental flosser" myself -- before that I always MEANT well, but...you know the excuses side-tracked types are prone too... )

Now don't get the wrong picture of our life -- we love variety and get a lot of it naturally, partly because of all the visiting we do and the good number of folks who visit us here at our farm.  I think now that once a family has a strong tradition about how they use time, has established regular rhythms a child can count on and look forward to, it also becomes just fine to "break tradition" for a time.  Take a vacation for a day -- or more.  We recently spent three hours straight in the afternoon reading aloud from a new book borrowed from the library (Molly was asleep in my lap the whole time...).  Math wasn't completed (or begun...), Jesse and Jacob didn't write a word all day, music was postponed.  We are free at home to go on these "binges" when something wonderful comes up.  Maintaining a basic rhythm to our days doesn't mean a bit of syncopation isn't a welcome delight.  Possibly the syncopation is even more special when the basic beat is strong... who knows.  And we always know our way of planning is there the next day, that we can take stock then of where we are and what we need to do.  It really is a trick, finding that balance between what rhythms help and give cohesiveness to our lives, and what is just an artificial and totally unhelpful cramping of your family's style. Probably it's most important to get out of the "punishment" frame of mind in structuring your time, but instead look at the ways you really want to USE your limited time well, for things that you truly feel are worth doing. The day we spent 3 hours reading aloud, THAT was what we most wanted to do. We wouldn't have had the heart for anything else.

We also usually find that we have much better days, have more of a good sense of accomplishment, if we all get up EARLY (of course, I hope you understand that we only KNOW this because of the contrast with the days when we're just groggily clearing up the breakfast dishes at 10:15...). Besides just being able to do more in the way of writing and reading or math work or music, if we're off to an early start the kids have more time to PLAY throughout the day, something they of course love. (Jesse is always careful now to plan in FREE time for himself, and not OVERplan his day...) If Jesse gets up early, he will sometimes read for a half-hour even before we have breakfast. And I'm still, whenever possible, arising before Molly to play piano for an hour or so in the lovely quiet of the morning, and I'm not half-bad now at most of the pieces in the Suzuki Book II. I suppose that that is indeed another tradition in our house -- waking up hearing Mommy playing piano downstairs. I think my kids would think it was odd now to begin the day any other way.

Perhaps one of the most positive things we've found about structuring our time well is that we then have the time to really accomplish things, and see improvement and growth. When I only played piano for scattered minutes here and there with Molly leaping up on my lap, it was very hard to see much progress. Once I made the regular commitment to early rising I've been really pleased to see my own learning moving along much faster. So too with the kids. Jacob has learned the rudiments of playing soprano recorder now -- because it's now a (happy!) tradition that we play recorder together every day, for at least a short bit -- complete with ritually marking his calendar after our playing times. (We even find it helps to have a special place to always play -- seems to help Jacob's concentration somehow.) Jesse is learning to read music for piano because we're working at it daily -- and together. Jesse is a writer because he WRITES regularly, and for his own purposes. We all can begin feeling good bursts of self-esteem from all these accomplishments, and feel motivated to continue and set new and higher goals. We can put stock in things a bit more, because we are more deeply involved in them, we're getting past the "just smattering" stage. (And we all have certainly "just smattered" in MANY things, and that is wonderful fun too, but really focusing is special in another way.)

I think that often we don't notice the real structure in our homeschooling and our family life, because it's just "what we do" and doesn't seem extraordinary or thought out or planned. Maybe indeed that is the sign that you've really found the right fit for your family -- when it all just seems natural, like no structure at all. Rather like a comfortable pair of shoes that you barely notice on your feet. The shoes are there, but they are a HELP to you, not a pinching or rubbing-the-wrong-way experience. And, too, just as shoes get old and too worn or too tight with age, and have to be discarded, so too we regularly need to reevaluate the condition of our family traditions and structures to see if the fit is still right. Make it a tradition, indeed, to change as we all grow.

# 12. What We Have Learned

Many parents find home education to be a learning experience for themselves, as well as for their children. This chapter is a summing up of some of the things that we have learned about how to best create a learning atmosphere in our home.

### Reading Aloud is the Foundation

Almost all our homeschooling activities begin with reading aloud. Our children have learned the alphabet partly by listening to alphabet books. They have been inspired to write from listening to other children's stories. They have become interested in arithmetic after hearing biographies of famous mathematicians. They have become connected to the past through reading stories and biographies of people who have lived in other times. We are raising children who love books.

### First Steps Must Not Be Rushed

Perhaps the biggest mistake made by schools is their rushing of children into reading. First graders in school who hardly know the alphabet get very frustrated when there are lots of words on a page. As a result they come to think of themselves as dumb, and they come to hate reading. At home, we allow reading to unfold at a slower pace. Once a child has begun to read, our cardinal principle is that the books should not be too hard. Hard books can be frustrating and overwhelming, and children don't learn when they are frustrated. (There is one exception to this rule: When children choose to read difficult books to themselves, they do not get frustrated by the hard words.)

There are a number of ways to determine before hand whether a book is difficult. Short words are easier to read, as are short sentences. Books with few words on a page are less intimidating. Large print is easier to read. Sometimes it is hard to find easy enough books. Since beginning reading textbooks often start off very easy, we often alternate between several different beginning reading textbooks when our children are first learning to read. As soon as possible, though, we've helped our children discover that they can read REAL books, not just "readers."

### Finding a Regular Rhythm

We have been almost surprised over the years to realize how helpful a definite but flexible structure can be in our homeschooling. I'm not even embarassed to tell people that, yes, we try to be quite organized in our time now. We can see our children responding positively to these expected traditions.

### Keep Sessions Enjoyable

We try to keep homeschooling times enjoyable so that our children will look forward to them. When our children make mistakes, we don't always correct them. Mistakes can be a good sign. or maybe just a sign that the child was answering a different question. The willingness to risk making mistakes -- just like when baby Hannah tries her darnedest to talk to us with her gurgles and oohs and ahhs -- is often the forerunner of success. Mistakes show that children are putting in the mental effort to figure things out. If children continue to put in the mental effort, and get the natural feedback of response and further modeling, the mistakes will eventually take care of themselves.

Children learn to talk without being corrected. A child who says "I *is* hungry" will eventually figure out how to say "I *am* hungry." When reading, a child who attends to meaning can notice when things don't make sense so that he can find his own mistakes. In writing, mistakes can be corrected on the second or third draft for essays that are being prepared for an audience. A computer word-processing system helps our children do second and third drafts because the whole piece does not have to be rewritten -- just the mistakes need to be changed.

When a child is reading or writing and comes to a word that he does not know, sometimes we will tell him the word, sometimes we help him figure it out, and sometimes we will tell him that we think he can figure it out himself. If a child is reading, and there is word after word in the text that he can't figure out on his own, then the book is too difficult.

The trick is to keep your child from getting frustrated while gradually increasing his independence. At first, when he is reading or writing or doing math, you are snuggling with him. He may be sitting on your lap or sitting right next to you. You are looking at the book or paper over his shoulder. You are telling him when you think he can figure out a word on his own. Gradually, you want to fade yourself out of the situation. You want to get to the point where you can be sewing or washing dishes or working with your other children and are just available to answer his questions. One home-schooling parent, Dan Wilcox, described this process as "getting out of your child's head." When you are telling your child whether or not he can figure out a word, you are telling him that you know what he can do better than he does. When you step aside you are telling him that you trust him to be in control of his own reading (or writing). If he asks you what a word is (or how to spell a word), there comes a time when you no longer say, "Try to sound it out yourself." There comes a time when you treat him just as you would an adult that would ask -- you answer him gracefully.

## Use Real Life Situations

Our children are motivated by real purposes. They will write letters that will really be sent, articles that will really be read, and books that will really be bound and treasured. They will add columns of numbers for real checkbooks and add up scores for real card games. One eleven year old took off into reading when she began to read to children that she was baby-sitting for. Many children read on a regular basis to their little brothers or sisters. Other children enjoy reading aloud on tape, and then sending the tape off to friends or family.

## Recognize Accomplishments

These days at supper Susan is always telling me what Jacob or Molly just read. I have to play a guessing game. When I guess all sorts of easy books incorrectly, they finally -- with great delight -- tell me what book it was. They appreciate my interest.

Another way we recognize our children's reading accomplishments is through our "stairways of books" where the kids write down the titles of books or chapters that they read. More important than any "gimmick" like that, though, is our readiness to discuss their books with them, share our feelings about them, listen to their retellings (Jesse's voice was breaking this morning as he told me about the ending of *Old Yeller*, and why he thought it was more similar to *Where the Red Fern Grows* than to the ending of *The Long Journey*).

We recognize their growing abilities in math by letting them take on real work that involves those skills. Jacob is proud that he gets to sort out the checks for our newsletter bank account as Jesse adds them all up.

### Establish a Collegial Relationship

We find we get on best with our children if we meet them as colleagues -- equal partners in learning, rather than know-it-all adults versus dumb kids. We share how we learn, how we solve problems, what types of books appeal to us, new insights we have into all subject areas -- and we listen to their ideas on the same things. We don't pretend we aren't adults who have been around a bit longer and so know a bit more, but we try to balance this with a readiness to see their thinking and hear their ideas. They often astonish us with their questions and insights.

**There is no audience more delightful to read for then homeschooled children. Our children chuckle out loud with delight at humorous passages in books that I read with them, and we just naturally stop and talk along the way, making remarks about the pictures or the story. There is an art to listening which home-schooled children just naturally pick up and that we might do well to emulate. When we listen to our children read or when we read their writing, we try to respond first to the story -- not just to their "errors." After all, they are patient with us when we are reading aloud and come across maybe a foreign word or a strange name that we don't know right off how to pronounce. They are patient with our stumbles.**

We share our writing with our children. We let them know that it takes us several drafts to get a letter or story written, and that we often heavily revise a piece or make mistakes along the way.

When they ask us questions, we don't pretend we know all the answers. Often our search together for answers helps our kids learn not only the answers, but also how to find answers. As colleagues in learning together, we share our children's vibrant interest in the world, past and present.

## In Sum

We have found that these approaches have worked positively with our own children.  (When we lapse into other ways of interacting, our kids let us know VERY quickly if it's NOT so positive!)  We hope we've spurred on some new thinking for you and your family, and that you'll find this adventure of learning with your kids to be worth the taking, and worth giving it your best.

# Notes

[1]J. Holt, *Escape from Childhood*, N.Y.: Ballantine Books, 1974, p. 134.

[2]D. Durkin, Is There a Match Between What Elementary Teachers Do and What Basal Reader Manuals Recommend? *The Reading Teacher*, 1984, *37*, 734-748.

[3]O. B. Speer, & G. S. Lamb, First Grade Reading Ability and Fluency in Naming Verbal Symbols. *The Reading Teacher*, 1976, *29*, 572-576.

[4]P. Satz, H. G. Friel, & J. Fletcher, Some Developmental and Predictive Precursors of Reading Disabilities: A Six Year Follow-up. In A. L. Benton & D. E. Pearl (Eds.), *Dyslexia: An Appraisal of Current Knowledge*. New York: Oxford University Press, 1978.

[5]R. J. Erion, Chronological Age, Immaturity, and the Identification of Learning Disability. *Educational Research*, 1986-1987, *11*, 2-7. Also Raymond S. Moore cites three other studies that came to the same conclusion that chronological age at school entrance is related to school success in R. S. Moore, Research and Common Sense: Therapies for Our Homes and Schools *Teachers College Record*, 1982, *84*, p. 367.

[6]D. Durkin, Is There a Match Between What Elementary Teachers Do and What Basal Reader Manuals Recommend? *The Reading Teacher*, 1984, *37*, 734-748.

[7]R. S. Moore, Research and Common Sense: Therapies for Our Homes and Schools *Teachers College Record*, 1982, *84*, 355-377.

[8]A. Huxley, *The Art of Seeing*, New York: Harper & Brothers, 1942; W. H. Bates, *Better Eyesight Without Glasses*, New York: Henry Holt and Company, 1920.

[9]J. Holt, *Never Too Late: My Musical Life Story*. New York:Delta/Seymore Lawrence, 1978 p. 131.

[10]L. I. Wilder, *On the Banks of Plum Creek* New York: Harper & Row, 1937, p. 152.

[11]J. Chall, *Learning to Read: The Great Debate*, New York:

McGraw-Hill, 1967, p. 307.

[12]H. T. Hahn, Three approaches to beginning reading instruction, ITA, language experience, and basal readers -- extended to second grade, *The Reading Teacher*, May 1967, *20)*, pp 711- 715

[13]N. Juster. *The Phantom Tollbooth*, New York: Epstein & Carroll, distributed by Random House, 1961, page 175.

[14]Jon Wartes, *Homeschooler Outcomes*, paper presented at the American Educational Research Association's National Conference, New Orleans, April 5, 1988.

[15]M. Botel, *A Comprehensive Reading Communication Plan* (Working Edition), Spring 1979, Pennsylvania Dept.     of Education, p.3.

[16]Ibid, p. 5.

# Pennsylvania Homeschoolers
## *Publishers*

**Writing from Home:** A Portfolio of Homeschooled Student Writing by Susan Richman, $8.95, 372 pages.

*Susannah Sheffer:* "More than a proud display of accomplishment... It is a way for us to begin to understand what makes accomplishment possible...."

*Home Education Magazine:* "An in-depth examination of the ways in which these children *learned* to write."

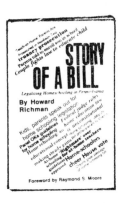

**Story of a Bill:** Legalizing Home-schooling in Pennsylvania by Howard Richman, $6.95, 152 pages.

This is the true story of how the homeschooling law was passed in Pennsylvania.

*Raymond Moore:* "You watch in awe as the drama unfolds."

*Mary Pride:* "The fast pace of a novel, the tension of a whodunit, and a happy ending!"

**Subscribe to *PA Homeschoolers***: If you want to find out the latest in the lives of the Richman family and read personal writing by other homeschooling parents and children, you might consider subscribing to *PA Homeschoolers*, our 32 page newsletter that comes out four times a year.

## Send for a free catalog from:
*PA Homeschoolers*
R.D. 2 -- Box 117
Kittanning, PA 16201
412-783-6512